A STRAIGHT BUYING
PROPERTY ABROAD

Steven Packer

Editor: Roger Sproston

www.straightforwardco.co.uk

Contents

*

**

Introduction

In the last 30 years or so, the world has shrunk considerably. Whereas not so long ago, most people, British and others, were buying property in Southern Europe, particularly France, Spain, Portugal and Italy, (with the exception of a few adventurous souls) nowadays virtually the whole of Europe is open thanks mainly to the proliferation of countries entering the European union. However, the situation in the next few years will change and the process of purchasing a property will alter as a result of the UK exiting the EU.

BREXIT is a wide reaching event that will affect not only the whole of the UK but potentially the wider world for years to come. one of the changes over the last three years, and particularly now in 2019, is the fluctuation and recent weakness of the pound against other currencies. This has made the process of purchase of overseas property inevitably more expensive. Another way that those looking to buy in Europe are likely to suffer from BREXIT is with regards to house deposits. EU citizens are charged smaller deposits than non-EU citizens. For example in France, minimum deposits for EU citizens are 20% of the full price whereas for non-EU citizens they can go up to as much as 50%.

Current owners of property could potentially lose out on some perks when the UK finally leaves the European Economic Area (EEA). An example of the perks include loss of tax breaks such as capital gains and gains on renting and selling which will increase for non-EU members.

Having said all that, there is an industry consensus that, in the short term, at least during the two year transition period, little will change for British buyers within the EU. In addition, people from all over the world buy properties within the EU so, whilst it may become a little more complex for Brits it will still be very possible. In addition, there will be no change in buyers costs.

So, having said all that, it is possible to buy a property, for leisure or for investment throughout the whole of Europe and also, thanks to ever cheaper air travel, in many countries throughout the world. Many people invest in countries where the climate is better than the UK, although just as many seem now to be investing in Eastern Europe, in search of culture rather than weather.

Other factors influencing would-be investors or those in search of a second home are stable interest rates and the low costs of borrowing money. Many hitherto inaccessible countries are now literally bending over backwards to make themselves attractive to foreign investors. An influx of foreign capital, along with foreign expertise is exactly what is needed now the old shackles have been removed and membership of the EU created the conditions for future prosperity. The average investment in property in the various EU countries is around £150,000, with lots of variations above and below that price. Whereas it was once mainly the elderly who desired that retirement home abroad, the mix of people buying abroad, for whatever reason, spans all age groups. Indeed, since property prices started to escalate to the absurd situation we have today (writing in 2019), especially in the south of England, and the cost of living has generally spiralled, many people have chosen to leave the UK in search of a better life.

This book aims to provide a general introduction to buying and selling property abroad. Many countries are covered. Obviously, for such a wide-ranging book, it is not possible to go into great depth about the legal and social systems in each country. The main aim is to introduce the systems peculiar to each country to hep give a flavour of property investment and what to look out for.

Many a dream has been shattered by the realties of different countries regimes covering property purchase. For sure there are estate agents now in most countries who will help guide a person through the maze. However, it has to be realised that those agents are also acting in their own interests. It is for this reason that a book such as this is highly pertinent in that it should provide pointers and highlight the possible pitfalls that lurk under the plethora of attractive advertisements that induce people to invest.

There are a number of more in-depth companion volumes to this book which explore in greater detail the processes of buying a home in a particular country. However, this book should provide a firm foundation for you to make up your mind and sort through the many options that you have.

Below are a few tips to ponder when thinking of buying a property abroad.

Buying off-plan

In the UK, a growth industry, corresponding to the opening-up of the property market, has been that of property exhibitions. Everywhere you go or look there are now property exhibitions selling the delights of property investment in just about every country that you can think of. Many of these exhibitions will be selling properties off- plan, i.e., before they are built. Clearly this is good for developers in that they have increased cash flow and guaranteed sales. The advantage for buyers, so it goes, is that by the time the property is ready the value will exceed what you paid for it. So you have an instant profit.

Before you buy a property off-plan you are required to have at least 20% deposit and also have all the necessary paperwork in place. You shouldn't forget that salespeople make hefty commissions out of those who buy off-plan and they will be using every trick in the book to ensure that they get your business. The scheme will have been heavily promoted and journalists will often be flown across to give a glowing review of the development.

It is vitally important that you have knowledge of the developer, the country in which the property is being purchased and the potential pitfalls. In many cases the property that you are purchasing may not be ready for several years. Will the developer still be in business? Remember they have your money! Always do your research before committing anything-do not be swayed by heavy selling and the pressure that comes with it.

Pitfalls to watch out for

Whether you are buying for investment or for leisure you don't want to end up poorer for the experience. There are a number of factors to consider and to bear in mind when buying a property abroad:

- Never believe that because a budget airline is either planning to, or has, introduced flights to a particular country that the price of property will rise. This is not the case and many airlines will introduce and then withdraw flights if they are not proving profitable;
- Always consider the associated costs when purchasing a property, what are the maintenance costs and what are local taxes and so on. Thorough research is necessary here before committing yourself;
- In particular, understand the tax regimes of a country before committing yourself. Some regimes are particularly harsh and you could also find yourself in a double tax situation, such as when/ if you choose to rent a property out.
- If you are hoping to rent a property out once purchased make sure that you do extensive research beforehand. Many developers are offering so called 'guaranteed rentals' to those who purchased property. Why should they do this if what they are offering is greater than the normal return? This is because, notwithstanding whether they can rent it for this guaranteed rental, the developer

has already factored this rental into the purchase price. Another gimmick!

- What are the conditions for selling the property. This is very important. Look for signs of over-development in a country, as has happened in Bulgaria and has certainly happened in Spain.

- What are the general conditions for obtaining a reasonable price for renovation in a country and what is the likelihood of getting ripped off. There are numerous websites which invite people to give their opinions of buying a property in a particular country and also offer the benefit of hindsight. There is a list of websites at the end of the book.

- Always try to view a property before you pay a deposit or buy. What you see in glossy brochures and on websites may not be the whole picture.

- What is the prospect for future growth? Again, get a clear picture of this very important aspect of investment. Don't rely on the headline figures in advertisements. Many countries are just as prone as we are to boom and bust cycles. Make sure that you have a clear investment plan before committing.

The Reasons to buy in a particular country

As we have seen, it is now possible to go anywhere almost, and to buy anything, almost. Property investment in a whole range of countries, to suit all pockets, has become the norm. However, it is very important to know yourself well and to know the reasons why you are about to invest in property in another country.

If you are not clear why you want to buy, but are attracted to the prospect of owning abroad, then the questions listed below are the ones that you should be asking yourself and reflecting on before making any move at all.

- What are you looking for in a property, do you want a second home, is it for investment and income/capital growth or a combination of these factors?
- Are you looking for an eventual retirement home?
- Is good weather an important factor?
- What do you know about a particular country and its future prospects?
- Will you become bored with a particular project after a time?

If you are planning to move permanently to another country can you make a living? How well do you know the language and customs of a country?

The point of asking these questions to yourself and to others involved in the project with you is to ensure that you are serious, know the upsides as well as the downsides and know yourself well. If you are choosing to go to another country to live make sure that you will want to be there in several years time. If you are buying a second home for holiday purposes, will you want to keep going back to the same place year in year out? Many who have invested in timeshare for example have found to their detriment that the novelty wears off after a while.

The main point to come out of the above is to be very careful, make sure that you know your country well before buying and never give in to sales pressure. Sales people are only your friend when you are lining their pockets. After that you are on your own.

The next chapter covers financing a purchase abroad, which underpins the whole process.

****

Chapter 1.

Financing a Purchase Abroad

Many in the UK traditionally levered equity out of their properties to finance their purchases abroad. Although this is still the case, currently the amount of people doing so has diminished. Many people will still look to the traditional route of raising a mortgage specifically to buy abroad.

The introduction of the euro altered the situation somewhat. It is now easier to compare prices within these countries when dealing with a single currency. However, at the same time this has resulted in a big demand for properties from Northern Europeans which has tended to drive prices upwards.

One factor that needs to be considered is that, no matter what the demand, it is highly unlikely, notwithstanding claims to the contrary from those advertising and selling property that property prices in Europe generally will see the illogical and ultimately damaging spiralling increases that characterised the UK property market. In fact, given the rapid new build development in European countries, it is likely that prices will go down as well as up, due to over-supply.

One other point to consider when purchasing abroad is the actual on-costs of purchasing a property. In most European countries the costs of purchasing are considerably higher than in the UK when factoring in costs such as legal fees, stamp duty (or the equivalent) and other taxes. These will be highlighted in the chapters dealing with individual countries.

Different ways of purchasing property abroad

There are two main ways of purchasing a property abroad, paying cash or raising a mortgage, much as in the UK. The mortgage can be raised either in the UK or abroad. There are a number of special mortgages that can be raised, usually in the country of purchase but also elsewhere raised by brokers.

As with the UK, especially now, you will have to prove to a foreign lender that you have sufficient income to repay a mortgage. They will ask for a large amount of proof, more so than UK banks, that this is the case Whether paying cash or buying on a mortgage you will need a bank account in the country where you purchase which must always be kept in credit.

There are advantages and disadvantages to paying in cash or by mortgage. With cash, of course you will not have to service a long-term loan which will end up costing you much more than the original purchase price of the property. However, when paying in cash, unless you are very careful, you could end up paying a lot for something that is not in fact worth the asking price.

When you get a mortgage at least the bank will wish to ensure that the collateral for their loan is secure. Hence they will insist on a thorough survey and will provide advice if the property in their opinion is not worth the price.

Disadvantages of overseas mortgages

It is worth mentioning here that there are several disadvantages to raising mortgages overseas. The main disadvantage is that it is in a foreign currency. This adds a relative layer of risk to your investment. With this set up, you are earning in sterling but paying in a foreign currency therefore you will be liable for any exchange rate fluctuations. Currently, at the time of writing, the pound is very weak against other currencies and costs will have gone up. There is also the disadvantage of communication barriers. You will need to visit the country at least once to sort out mortgage matters and you will find barriers which could impact on anything you do or sign.

It is entirely up to you how you raise capital but bear in mind the disadvantages.

Most mortgage lenders will insist that a property has the proper insurance and also many will want you to have life insurance. Remember that they are lending money against a property and against your income and they wish to be safe and see their loan protected. When paying cash it is up to you what you do although most people would take the sensible route and make sure insurance is in place.

When buying a foreign property on a mortgage you will have to have a mortgage inspection report, and pay for this. This is non-refundable and can cost anything up to £600. A qualified surveyor will prepare the report and submit this to the lender. From this report the lender will decide whether or not there is enough security in the property to justify the mortgage being asked for.

Once satisfactory reports have been received you will be offered a loan, in writing, and an offshore company may be set up for the sole purpose of owning the property. This is a convenient way for the banks to lend to a person to buy property in another country.

One typical mortgage arrangement for buying a property abroad is that of Santander UK who will loan up to 75% of the purchase price for property in Spain or Portugal. As in the UK the more you borrow the more you pay. This will exclude legal and other fees which you must find yourself. It is purely against the property. Loans can be arranged for a variety of residential purchases, main residence, second home, buy to let ad so on. However, they will not lend on commercial property. For mortgages on French, Portuguese and Italian properties the process is similar. However, in some countries, such as Italy and Portugal, you will need to hand over around one third of the purchase price. One thing to watch out for is when buying in Spain, the buyer will be saddled with any debts of the seller on completion of purchase.

Lloyds TSB lends money for purchase of property in a range of countries, including France, Spain, Portugal and the US. the minimum you can borrow is £100,000, or the currency equivalent. Barclays lends for properties in France, Spain, Italy and Portugal.

When looking at property, particularly in Spain or Portugal, where many people have suffered the adverse effects of property laws, you will need to satisfy yourself of the following:

- Are there any major works required on the property and what will the costs be? Are all the services connected? This may sound silly but this is quite often the case when you purchase new build in these countries.
- What will be the impact of future developments on your property. Although the massive development programmes, which has led to over development and price falls, in Spain has now slowed it is still important to carry out thorough searches before committing. The property with sea views that you purchased could turn out to be a property with a view of brick walls.
- Is the property within a community development or urbanization scheme which would make community fees payable?

If you are purchasing a property in euros then the monthly payments must also be in euros and these funds must be cleared so that they are available on each repayment date. Whether making payments in euros or sterling your bank account must always be in credit at least two months payments.

Mortgages in Spain and Portugal are typically available for 75% of the purchase price There will be an administration fee to the lender of around £300-£350 refundable only if your application is turned down. Valuation fees, as in the UK, are not refundable. If buying on a mortgage you will be responsible for the lenders legal fees as well as your own. These will typically be around 1% of the purchase price but could vary.

Wherever you are buying, you need to provide the following information to mortgage companies:

- Three years tax returns
- P60's for three years
- Payslips for a determined period, usually six months
- If self-employed letters from your accountant
- Three items of credit, such as Visa, Amex etc
- Evidence of mortgage history
- Two reference letters, one from your bank
- Three months bank statements
- Copy of your passport.

Basically, banks abroad are very stringent, much more so than UK banks. You will also need to open a bank account in the country where you wish to buy. Six months mortgage payments must be in this account when the property is purchased.

There are a few other things that it is important to know when purchasing abroad. Check the VAT levels in different countries as sometimes there is a high VAT level levied on new build properties which can raise the purchase price considerably. Check on-costs thoroughly as these are not always advertised by over enthusiastic estate agents. The rule of thumb when buying abroad is that you should add around 10% of the price when working out costs.

There are many mortgages around, although as we are seeing these are diminishing, as the true state of the economy is emerging following the onset of the credit crunch. Nevertheless if you are a solid bet you will always get a mortgage.

Using currency brokers

There are many specialist currency brokers around who state that they can achieve a better rate than mainstream banks. Currency brokers buy currency in large amounts so that they can secure better rates than the mainstream banks. Specialist currency brokers will discuss with you the best ways of financing your purchase abroad. If the dealer knows the proposed date of purchase they can then tell you the best rates available at the time. As there are plenty of dealers around you can shop around until you are satisfied that you have the best rate. When you have chosen you then sign a currency contract which will usually entail a fee of around £20-30.

Most ordinary people are now using currency brokers rather than banks to buy properties. If you do intend using such a company then you will need to carry out basic checks of your own before committing:

- Make sure that the company has at least three years audited accounts
- Use a company that specialises in foreign exchange only
- Make sure that the person you are dealing with is a trained broker as the usual high pressure techniques exist in this field as they do elsewhere
- Always get a number of quotes

When buying a property abroad you should bear in mind that even quite small fluctuations in exchange rates can significantly affect the total purchase price of a property.

Taxes

All properties abroad are subject to local taxes, as in the UK. Income declared from rent is taxable. UK residents letting out a property abroad will be liable for UK income tax. Taxes are payable only once so there won't be a double whammy. However, even if tax is not due a return must be made to the authorities in respective countries.

When the property is sold it will be subject to capital gains tax unless it is your own principal home. For details of capital gains tax you should contact HM Revenue and Customs. As a rough guide, if you have owned the home for 10 years 60% of the gain is payable. However, you should contact HMRC for information, as this area is more complex than most people think.

The UK has tax treaties with many countries which allow for exemption from foreign tax as long as this is paid in the UK.

Inheritance tax

If you own a property abroad then inheritance tax matters have to be addressed. Before buying a property abroad you will need sound advice. Generally speaking, it is better to put a property in joint names because in most countries other than the UK, inheritance tax is charged on property passed between spouses. In the UK, property can pass between one married partner to another without incurring this tax. If you wish to put your children's name on the property or set up a limited company or trust fund make sure you have good legal advice before you do this. Discover in advance how inheritance tax operates in each country as these differ. For example, in some countries now emerging as desirable locations women are not allowed to own property. This is the case in Islamic countries. If you are interested in buying in an Islamic country find out how these laws will affect you and your inheritance tax position.

You will also need to know whether your foreign property forms part of your UK estate. For example in Spain, Portugal and Italy, as a foreigner you can leave your property according to the rules in your native country. However, in France, Dubai and Turkey even as a foreigner you must abide by the rules of that country. This means for instance that you cannot cut out your children and there is no automatic tax-free inheritance between husband and wife. On buying a foreign property you should make both a new English will and a will that is valid in the country where you have your property.

Different types of market abroad

Markets abroad can be split into three: primary, secondary and tertiary. Primary markets are sophisticated and long established, have a well-developed infrastructure and are places where foreigners have successfully bought property for many years. Secondary markets are less well established, legal structures are not developed and are places where foreigners have only just started to buy. The risks are higher but the returns can be correspondingly higher. Examples of secondary markets are Croatia, Turkey and Dubai.

Tertiary markets are countries or areas where purchase by foreigners has become recently possible, but is not at all established. Properties in tertiary markets will appear to be very cheap but the infrastructure of these countries is very fragile or unknown and the buying process can be very difficult for a number of reasons: the title to land is unclear or may be disputed. Mortgages may not be available and the paperwork may not be valid. These brand new markets represent the highest risk for a potential purchaser.

Examples of tertiary markets at the time of writing include Poland, Slovakia, Russia and the Czech Republic. Over time these market will develop but beware when purchasing or looking to purchase a property as there are currently many pitfalls. Get good advice, Go onto the numerous websites which give case histories of people who have bought.

Fractional ownership

Fractional ownership is a relatively new scheme whereby you purchase a fraction of the title deed. Fractional ownership is different to timeshare or holiday clubs where membership is purchased but no title deed. This type of ownership is best suited to holiday homes that are intended to be used for four to six weeks a year. You will get a corresponding share of the title deed entitling you to a certain time. These types of property are typically situated in luxury holiday complexes with sports facilities, such as golf. The management fee payable will also be correspondingly lower as more people are sharing. One point to consider if looking at this type of ownership is that the property is never really yours.

****

Chapter 2

Buying in France

France and Spain are the most popular and established countries for UK buyers. France was given a huge push by the arrival of the Euro tunnel and also by the introduction of pet passports.

France has much to recommend it. It is by far the easiest and cheapest country to get to for British people and we are used to French culture. Many of us have even mastered the language. The vast majority of people who buy in Spain do so as a lifestyle choice rather than for investment. Property prices in France do not rise significantly enough for people to speculate in the short term. Whatever is done is in the longer term.

There are very many nice properties in France and you can buy anything from a run down barn to a gorgeous farmhouse. The average price paid by UK citizens for a property in France in 2019 was £200,000. There are many variations above and below that price. In recent years the price of property in France has reduced significantly, seeing falls of up to 18% in value. However, they are now on the rise again. There are many cultural diversities throughout France. If you want a property in the remote villages there are plenty on offer. If you fancy your chances in the wine growing regions thee are plenty on offer. France overall is a beautiful country and it is not surprising that many people, fed up with the UK, move lock stock and barrel to France.

You need to think about where you would buy in France and why. Do you want to be nearer the sea or inland? Near to the UK or far way? Transport links are generally good, particularly with the advent of budget airlines but you can sill travel long distances to get to your second home. The weather is another factor. Normandy for example sees many inches of rainfall each year whilst Provence can get below freezing at night

Once you have discovered an area that you are happy with, on all fronts, there will be other decisions to make. Most people buying a second, or permanent home in France prefer old to new houses. However, you may be faced with renovation costs and also faced with dealing with builders who you do not know or cannot fully trust. If you are planning to embark on renovation ensure that you have sourced a good architect who is very familiar with the system. In addition, think about your time. In many cases, you will have to travel at weekends or holiday time to carry out renovations, unless you have moved permanently out there. This can become expensive and tedious. What was originally your dream could go wrong. Make sure you know what you are doing before doing it and don't sweep uncomfortable questions or decisions under the table.

Pet passport schemes are now available for many countries, including France, and the cost of preparing your pet for its excursion abroad is about the same as two weeks in kennels or a cattery. Your pet will have to be micro-chipped, implanted with a permanent radio frequency device for identification and have anti- rabies injections and blood tests. It is quite a lot of work and it is worth discussing it with your vet or logging on to petsabroad.uk.com for an information pack.

When it comes to retiring to France, ever more people are doing so. If you have retired and are in receipt of a state pension, this can be paid straight into your French bank account. How much you receive will depend on the exchange rate so it may be subject to some fluctuation. Your pension could be liable to French rather then UK taxation. You need to complete all the relevant paperwork but in the end may benefit due to lower French tax rates.

However, if you are in receipt of a government pension, such as civil service or police, you will be required to pay UK and not French tax. For details on pensions you should contact the International Pension Centre On 0191 218 7777 or www.gov.uk/international-pension-centre. Those in private pension schemes should contact their providers.

The process of buying a property in France

Buying a property in France is a different process to that of the UK with the involvement of different personnel. The average length of time is roughly equivalent to that of the UK, between two to three months, depending on whether you are paying cash or have a mortgage.

The main person involved in property transactions is the Notary. The notary is a public servant, legally qualified who represents the vendor and the purchaser. The purchaser pays the notaries costs, between 7% to 8% of the purchase price.

The notary's job is to make all the relevant searches, notify the authorities, draw up the draft deed of sale and look into any other areas, such as rights of way, planning permissions and also to ensure that there are no outstanding charges or arrears on the property. Purchasing a French property involves two contracts. The first is a preliminary sales contact, which can be dawn up in the UK and can be witnessed by an estate agent. On signature of the preliminary contract the purchaser has to pay 10% of the purchase price, which will be deducted on signature of the final deed. If the purchaser changes his or her mind the deposit is forfeited. If, by contrast, any conditions included in the contract are not fulfilled the deposit is refunded.

There will be other payments in between the preliminary contract and completion. Transaction fees charged by the estate agent will be between 5 and 10% of the purchase price. There are notary's fees and also disbursements, duties, taxes, searches and mortgage registry if applicable. VAT may have to be paid on properties under five years old if not previously sold.

Once you own the property you will be liable for local property taxes, plus occupancy taxes if you live in the property. You will also be liable for French taxes once you sell the property or if you let it and derive income. French tax may also be due if you die whilst still owning the property. As soon as you become the owner you will need to open a French bank account to pay for the utilities.

There is a scheme operating in France where it is possible to buy a home in instalments from an elderly person who is not expected to live much longer. It is not that well known in Britain. This is known as *la vente en viager*. This type of sale is usually arranged when the owner wants to raise capital whilst remaining in the property, a form of equity release. The buyer will pay an initial lump sum and then regular instalments for the rest of the owner's life. The upside of this scheme is that the future owner does not have to pay the full price of the property all at once. The risk is not knowing how long the current owner will live. It is important to look into inheritance tax liabilities of this scheme before entering into it.

New build projects in France

Most people when thinking of a French property think of an old property with character, such as a farmhouse or an old detached property. However, there are a lot of new build properties for sale. Quite often, new build properties, particularly flats are more secure than old houses left empty for long periods of time. The position of the would be purchaser of a new build property has improved in France in relation to VAT. Previously, a purchaser buying a property less than five years old, which was purchased as a new building, would be charged VAT, whether the seller was registered for VAT or not. A resale on the property within the five years would leave the seller having to pay VAT but not the purchaser. So, for a purchaser, this could be a double-whammy.

The position changed from 31st December 2012. From that date, only people registered for VAT could charge VAT on the sale. This saves purchasers of new-build property a significant amount of money. In addition, on a second sale, no VAT is paid at all, by the seller although the purchaser has to pay stamp duty of 5.09%. This side of the tax situation needs investigating carefully if you are thinking of buying new build.

Stamp duty generally

For properties more than 5 years old, stamp duty is 5.8%, or 5.09% in some departments. For properties less than 5 years old, stamp duty is 0.7% plus VAT at 20%.

Other VAT considerations

It is possible to get VAT refunded to you from the tax administration (or taken off the asking price when purchasing) if you are planning to rent your property furnished on a short term basis with rental services.

This letting activity is considered as commercial activity allowing you therefore to claim the VAT. The conditions are quite simple:

- you need to rent your property furnished

- on a short term basis

- at least 3 'para-hotel' services have to be offered to the tenants i.e. reception (handover of the keys), bed and linen changing, cleaning & breakfast (it can just be a breakfast delivery)...

Many high street rental management agencies propose these lease options to owners, especially in the French Alps. You just need to make sure you sign a flexible commercial lease agreement with them which also enables you to also use the property as you want.

The rental agency will manage, maintain and rent the property on your behalf. You will be of course free to use your property whenever you want (you'll just need to tell the agency before the beginning of the ski season when you are planning to occupy your property).

Payments and Rebates

If you are buying a new-build property which has already been completed, you must pay the full property price including VAT and then you will get the VAT back 3 to 6 months after the signature.

If you buy off plan, the VAT can sometimes be taken off the property price at the start of the purchase. Alternatively, as off-plan properties are normally paid for in stage payments, you pay each stage payment including VAT and then get refunded the VAT accordingly on each stage payment.

The VAT rebate is being provided on the basis that the property is being rented over 20 years, which means you have to rent your property during that period

Selling your property

As you own the freehold title of the property it is possible for you to resell your property before the end of the 20-year period. As the property is being managed by a rental company, there are a few important things to remember:

- If you resell the property and the new purchaser carries on the rental activity there won't be any VAT to repay as the VAT will keep on being rebated with the new purchaser.

- If you resell the property after year 10 for example and the new purchaser does not want to carry on with the lease activity, you may have to repay 50% of the VAT that you received initially.

Selling a property 'Plus Values' or Capital Gains Tax

This tax, known as capital gains tax in English, is charged on the difference between the purchase price and the selling price. There are various exemptions (see the section below).

The rate is currently 34.5% of the difference between buying and selling price. That's technically comprised of 19% income tax and 15.5% social levies.

Non-EU residents used to be charged a different rate but this is no longer the case since 2015.

On gains greater than €50,000, a supplementary tax is charged on top of the above, rising from 2% to 6% for extremely large gains.

A good website which gives an in depth breakdown of costs incurred when buying a property in France is https://transferwise.com/us/blog/property-tax-in-france.

Another good site is:

https://englishspeakingrealestateagentsfrance.com

Buy to let

There is a thriving rental market in France's main tourist areas. However, the season for letting is short so it is very difficult indeed to make any money out of property, let alone cover costs. Many areas in France have no letting potential at all, so if this is your idea then you need to carry out in depth research before committing yourself to buying. As a general rule, older properties that have been renovated are more popular and easier to let than new developments. Obviously, if you are buying in a city such as Paris then year round lets are very possible, as they are in London, particularly to students. As with everything, research the background to letting properties, look at demand and always look at the tax situation.

When buying a property in France, beware of those places that can only be reached by a budget airline. As we mentioned earlier small airlines are always vulnerable and can collapse or be bought at any time, leaving you with a problem. In addition, approach the purchase of any French property with extreme care and caution. There is a proliferation of websites with properties on offer for less than £10,000. As the average price of a house is £100,000 this is cheap. Why is it so cheap? Basically, the picturesque barn or cottage on offer at a low price will almost certainly need complete rebuilding.

France is a big country with over 2 million empty properties (compared to 150,000 in the UK). There are many cheap properties and many, many people who buy them and find their selves in a mess. The price of the land is almost worthless, so what exactly are you buying? This end of the market is for those who are serious about renovating, not for the average buyer.

Inheritance tax

French inheritance tax law is complicated, more so than the UK. Unlike the UK, each person under French law has their own tax free allowance, which differs depending on the relationship between them and the deceased. Currently, French inheritance tax varies from zero to 60%. An inheritance tax-free allowance of about 100,000 euros is available to any child of the deceased with 20% above that or more depending on the wealth of parents (figures as at 2019).

French healthcare

For those who are thinking of spending periods in France or moving lock stock and barrel, the French healthcare system is one of the best, if not the best in Europe. The system consists of a private/public partnership whereby part of the cost of medical treatment is paid by social security and the remainder by the individual. In order to make the system work efficiently, French social security contributions are high, as much as 18-20% of net income. Retired UK citizens living permanently in France can receive the same benefits as French nationals, as long as they have worked in an EU country. The form E121/S1, available from the pensions office in Newcastle upon Tyne, is necessary to register.

You should bear in mind that all of this will probably change when the process of leaving the EU is completed. Those who are not French residents will have to pay first then apply for reimbursement through their own social security system. Those living in France either permanently or for long periods should take out private insurance. For short stays in France, the form E121, stamped and signed by your local post office enables you to receive medical treatment under a reciprocal agreement with the UK. It lasts for three months. However, even in cases such as this it is still advisable to have private insurance.

*

Useful addresses and websites

The below represent a cross section of sites dealing with all aspects of buying property in France.

Anglo French Law-specialist legal advice
0333 335 6767

The legal process
https://www.french-property.com/guides/france/purchase-real-estate/.

Hamptons International-general sales information

hamptons-international.com

French Property News-deals with all aspects of property in France

www.completefrance.com

www.french-property.com

Financial information related to French property purchases

French property buying generally

Frenchentree.com

Rightmove

www.rightmove.co.uk/overseas-property/France-guide.html

www.francebuyingguide.com

****

Chapter 3

Buying in Spain

Buying in Spain has long been a favourite for UK citizens seeking to buy a home abroad, either for holidays or for retirement.

The Spanish property market

Spain was badly affected by the global financial crisis and resulting property market crash, with house prices dropping by as much as 30%. Nearly a decade on, there are signs that the recovery is finally underway, with indices showing year-on-year price increases in major cities and resorts, and an overall national rise of 4% in 2017.

Transaction numbers are increasing too, with data from the National Institute of Statistics showing sales increased by 16% in 2017.

Home ownership levels are high in Spain, with around 80% of residents owning their own home, and many doing so outright, without a mortgage.

Spain has a wide choice of properties for sale, either new, second-hand or old, there is guaranteed sunshine in most parts of the country all year round, it is cheap, familiar and is a primary country, as mentioned earlier. There are communities of ex-patriots, if this is what is wanted and there are also reasonable rental possibilities, in certain areas.

Whereas many buyers used to go (and still do) to the Costa's, and originally to places such as Benidorm, nowadays the trend has changed with many people choosing to live in Andalucia (particularly Marbella and the surrounds) and other areas up and down Spain. Many migrants come to Spain because of lower property prices and guaranteed sun, although water shortages in Spain are becoming more prevalent. There are 39 airports in Spain and a very developed road network which makes it easy to enter Spain and to get around.

Should you rent or buy in Spain?

Rental opportunities can be limited in some parts of Spain. One estate agency has claimed that rent prices in Spanish cities have increased by as much as 15% in a year, and that this can partially be attributed to the growing popularity of short-term holiday lets through websites such as Airbnb.

Now, some authorities in Spain are already seeking to curb this trend, with Madrid set to bring in new rules in 2019 to regulate the holiday let sector.

The BREXIT effect

As we discussed in the introduction, it is business as usual for British people wishing to buy a property in the EU, at least until after the two year transition period following the formal withdrawal on October 31st 2019. However, keep up to date with the situation on an ongoing basis.

The process of buying in Spain

Spanish property transactions tend to move a lot quicker than in the UK and again it is a notary (who is not a qualified solicitor) who oversees the purchase or sale. The overall cost of buying in Spain is around 12% of purchase price which covers legal costs and other expenses.

The process of buying a property in Spain usually runs as follows. First, the buyer makes an offer, usually through the seller's estate agent. If this is accepted, then the buyer and seller sign a preliminary contract (*contrato privado de compravento*) and the buyer pays a deposit, typically 10% of the purchase price.

The buyer then arranges any mortgage they require, although they should have already discussed their needs with the mortgage provider. The contract of sale (*escritura de compravento*) is usually signed in front of a notary, at which point the full sale price, taxes and other costs become due.

Legal requirements

The services of a notary are not legally required to complete the sale, but it is advisable and required by many mortgages.

The seller is responsible for hidden defects in the property, even if they are not aware of them. However, in practice gaining restitution for such defects can be difficult and costly.

Paying the costs and taxes associated with buying a home can be completed by the buyer or their agent. It is the buyer's responsibility, however, to ensure taxes are paid.

The buyer is also responsible for registering the property. The notary may provide this service for a fee, and/or may notify the registry office that the sale has taken place, without completing full registration.

Funding purchase: deposits and mortgages

Following the 2008 crash, Spanish banks were reformed with significant IMF involvement. This reduced the number of lenders in operation, and significantly increased the regulation and oversight of the industry. As a result, many banks began to lend less and mortgage rates and terms became less favourable.

Mortgage lenders will not complete on a mortgage agreement until you own a property. For this reason, it's important to include a clause in the contract allowing you to exit the agreement if you cannot acquire a mortgage.

Fees and charges

Costs are primarily paid by the buyer, and vary from region to region. Many are negotiable – there are no fixed fees for lawyers or estate agents. Costs paid by the buyer include:

- Property transfer tax 6–10% (existing properties) / VAT (or IVA) at 10% (new properties);
- Notary costs, title deed tax and land registration fee 1–2.5%;

- Legal fees 1–2% (including VAT).

The estate agent's fees are usually paid by the seller, and this is typically their only cost. Estate agents usually charge a percentage, typically around 3% of the final sale price.

Capital gains tax

Capital gains tax is paid on the profit of selling your home, i.e. the difference between the listed purchase price and the listed sale price, and the level in Spain currently varies between 19% and 23%.

First €6,000 – 19%

€6,000 – €50,000 – 21%

€50,000+ – 23%

Thus if you pay €200,000 for a property and sell it for €350,000 you will pay capital gains tax on €150,000. Due to the tiered system this would add up to €33,260 euros.

You may be able to claim a reduction on the capital gains tax to account for inflation; or if you are purchasing another property in Spain; or if you are over 65 and have lived in the property as your main residence for more than three years.

Otherwise, unlike in other countries, capital gains tax applies no matter how long you've lived in the property. Your residential status does not affect the application of capital gains tax either, as capital gains tax should be paid in Spain for property owned in Spain even if you are no longer a resident.

Choosing a reliable lawyer

Any lawyer practising in Spain should be registered with the local bar association (*Colegio de Abogados*).

They will have a registration number that you can ask for and then verify with the bar association. Naturally, registration does not guarantee honesty or competence, but it is a good minimum standard to insist on.

You can find a list of all the bar associations at the national website for Spanish lawyers, <u>Abogacía Española</u>.

Finding a translator

Many governments provide lists of lawyers and translators who speak both Spanish and another language. The British Embassy has a list of translators a useful resource.

The Spanish government also provides a list of accredited translators.

Debts transfer with property

In Spain, any mortgage or debt tied to a property is transferred to the new owner when the property is sold. It's thus critically important to ensure that there are no debts attached to the property when it is sold, or that if there are, they are covered by the terms of the contract. Debts may include:

- A mortgage;
- payments due to a tenant's association;
- property tax (*impuesto sobre bienes inmuebles*).

There are legions of people who have suffered adversely following the purchase of a property in Spain, indeed in many cases their lives have been ruined.

It is very important to check and double-check everything to do with a purchase before committing yourself.
In many areas the Spanish authorities are a law unto themselves and seem to do what they want. It has been common for property owners to arrive back at their property after a spell away to find it partly demolished or for a developer to have built right in front of their home ruining their views. It is a slow and painful process trying to find justice in these situations.

As there are now thousands of agents and others in the UK offering property for sale it is vitally important to get good advice. Such advice can be obtained from the Federation of Overseas Property Developers (FOPDAC) who may advise on planning problems but only if the developer is a member (see back for useful contacts).

Buying off-plan
Be especially careful here. One thing to note is a Spanish Supreme Court ruling in December 2015 which means that if you bought a property off plan that isn't delivered on time by the developer, and they have since gone bankrupt, you can reclaim your money back from the bank which was meant to safeguard your deposit. Nevertheless you should always guard yourself from any unnecessary grief.

While malicious intent is rare, caution is advised when buying a property which does not yet exist. At minimum you should:

- Check the company exists and is officially registered; check online at www.registradores.org (Spanish only).
- Ensure that the project is registered with the land registry.
- Check that planning permission has been granted by enquiring at the local city hall.
- Not sign a contract you don't understand.
- Ensure that any translation is done by an independent party.
- Demand proof that any sums paid (e.g. a deposit) are being held or spent appropriately.
- Get proof that you'll get a refund of your money if the property is not built.

As a non-resident, you may also buy land and have a property built yourself. In this case, good legal advice is even more important as you will need to ensure that contracts with builders are appropriate and watertight.

What are you looking for from a home in Spain?

There are many types of property on sale in Spain to suit every taste. You can, of course, get the newer types of home up and down the coast, on the Costa's and elsewhere but you can also get villas and farmhouses and other older type properties inland.

The older houses will require renovation and this should be factored into your budget. More and more people are choosing to buy property for investment in Spain and letting these properties out. However, the problems with the property market and the advent of other destinations such as Croatia have tended to slow this trend somewhat, but not completely stifle it. As usual, with property recessions, one person's loss is another person's gain, particularly those who choose to invest for the longer term.

If you are considering an investment-only purchase in Spain, choose the area very carefully. The property has to be near airports, swimming pools and beaches and have good access by road. Other factors to look at when buying for investment are what are the service charges, is the property well constructed and free of damp and what will the property look like in the future, i.e. how well will it age?

A note of caution.

Many developers offer fly and buy trips for would be purchasers. Although many treat these trips as a cheap holiday, once you arrive at the airport you will be assigned a representative who will stick to you like a leech and won't let go until you sign on the dotted line. If you don't, you will be put on the next flight home and will be expected to pay for the flight yourself. If you do plan to go on one of these trips then make sure that you go for an established developer. Look at other developments by the same developer. Look closely at the market for future resale and also what other developments are planned for the area.

Have you researched the true value of the property, are you getting the best deal?

Health and social security in Spain

Many people retire to Spain and have been doing so for years, looking to relocate to warmer climes and to start a new life, hopefully more leisurely. Retirement homes and developments are very popular and cheaper than they were. They are available to those over 70 and they usually have medical and dental clinics within the complex, plus nursing care and shopping facilities. However, they do come at a price and the service charges are always quite high as they are in the UK to pay for the range of facilities available.

Free health care is generally available to those who pay into Spanish social security. Otherwise it is essential to have private health insurance. If you are planning to live in Spain permanently then you may not get a residents permit without it.

Many Britons retire to Spain in the belief that they will be entitled to the same level of health care that they receive at home. This is not the case. They may be ineligible for medical treatment in Spain but too ill to qualify for full private insurance. In this case they will not be entitled to free health care unless the correct forms are filled in beforehand. It is highly recommended that private insurance is taken out if you intend to relocate to Spain. If you are semi-resident in Spain, living there, for example, for six months every year you can domicile your health care in one country only and you would need to arrange insurance in the other country.

As with other things, do your research before committing yourself.

The Canary Islands

If it is sun all the year round that you are after, and mainland Spain cannot fit the bill then the Canary Islands are for you. However, even the Canary Islands cannot guarantee all year round sun, with parts of the Canaries, such as Lanzarote being very windy

Over the last two decades the Canaries have been over-developed, with time-share scammers moving into the area. The Canaries have become, according to some, the same nightmare as the Spanish Costa's, i.e. miles of concrete hotels with masses of bored tourists mingling around the place. The Lonely Planet Guide had this to say about the Canaries:

"The Canaries are a seething mass of oily flesh jiggling in the lap of the waves and to the beat of discos, bars and gay nightclubs. They offer the worst of mass tourism: concreted shorelines, tacky apartment block after tacky apartment block and bars where you can pretend that you have never left home".

It is not all mass tourism though. Beyond the mega-resorts you can still find tiny fishing villages, whitewashed hamlets perched on hilltops and even a few wild places within the dull roar of a volcano or with mist dripping through primeval forests.

You certainly won't be treading where no one has trod before, but the Canaries pack enough into seven islands to suit all tastes.

The overall capital is Las Palmas Gran Canaria, and the major industry is tourism. There are apartments and villas for sale on all the islands. Gran Canaria is the most developed of all the islands and has many beaches. Tenerife, perhaps the most well known is the biggest of the seven islands and also has a dry and arid climate, with the north being lusher and humid. Tenerife is the most highly developed and is the island most full of tacky flats, cheap package tours and rip off time-shares. Like all of Spain, the Canaries are feeling the crunch and prices have dropped considerably over the last five years.

Las Palma is the must humid and luxuriously landscaped of all the islands and is green and full of woodlands. La Gomera, near the equator has trade winds and cool currents.

Fuerteventura is one of the most interesting of the Canary Islands because it is less developed than the others. Because of the rampant over-development of the other islands the Spanish government stepped in just in time to prevent the same ugly rash. As a result there are no high rises and the place is a magnet for wind and sea surfers. Fuerteventura means 'windy island'. There is virtually no rainfall and a permanently strong wind. The biggest attraction for tourists and settlers, of all the Canaries, is the dry heat. For this reason many Europeans with health conditions will settle there. For serious watersport enthusiasts and those wishing to escape cold damp dark European nights, the Canaries have much to offer.

Useful information

Estate agents

Hamptons International (Offices in several parts of Spain)

168 Brompton Road

London SW3 1HW

020 7589 8844

e-mail international@hamptons-int.com

www.hamptonsinternational.co.uk

www.spainbuyingguide.com/buying-in-spain/viewing-guide/the-estate-agent

Lawyers

https://www.solicitorsinspain.com

https://www.gov.uk/government/publications/spain-list-of-lawyers

websites

www.buy-spanish.co.uk

www.barclays.co.uk

www.propertysalespain.co.uk

https://www.aplaceinthesun.com/spain

Canaries

The Property Finders

www.thepropertyfinders.com

4

Buying in Portugal

Portugal has become the third most popular European country for those in search of a second home or those wishing to relocate permanently. There are price ranges to suit most pockets although it must be said that the presence of high profile celebrities on the islands, and their deep pockets, has pushed the prices up considerably.

Portugal is only a two and a half hour flight away, its climate is very similar to Spain and because of rigorous planning restrictions it hasn't been spoiled by rashes of ugly high-rise blocks of hotels and apartments. The pace of life is slower and more relaxed and the country as a whole is more up market than Spain.

The British population is quite considerable with around 200,000 Brits at the last count. Living costs are quite low and there is no inheritance tax. Sports are quite popular in Portugal with well developed golf courses. There is a 'golden triangle' of Quinta do Lago, Vale de Lobo and Via Sol, all within an hour's drive of Faro airport where new villas go for over £1m. In many of these developments over 90% of occupants are British which means that there is a familiar way of life with year round weather and year round golf.

If you are interested in buying in Portugal then you will need to decide whether buying into a complex is what you want or whether you would prefer the peace and quiet of an authentic Portuguese village. Prices are a lot lower, but they are harder to find and maintain and to get to.

Getting to Portugal is easy. Flights are cheap and competitive with cut-price airlines offering cheap deals to Faro and Lisbon. Again, the low cost of these flights are affected by the problems of oil prices, although they still remain competitive.

Financing a purchase in Portugal

Mortgages on property in Portugal are arranged on the same lines as Spain. Many lenders insist that properties must be bought through the medium of an off-shore company. This is taken care of by the lender. Mortgages are available in euros or sterling and are for up to 65% of the value of the property. Santander, for example, will lend a minimum of 100,00 euros. There is a non-refundable charge of £500 which includes the cost of valuation. On top of that there will be costs for legal fees and an arrangement fee. You will need to submit exhaustive documentation, bank statements, three-months payslips, proof of identity and latest mortgage statements for any current mortgages. Self-employed people have to provide four years of audited accounts.

As far as health care is concerned the same caution has to be applied as with Spain. Although Portugal has a National Health Service it is renowned for its inefficiency. Most foreign nationals take out private health care insurance. Those who have retired to Portugal and are in receipt of a state pension are entitled to the same level of health care as native Portuguese. Doctors are trained to the same standard as the UK but tend to be more inefficient.

Investing in property in Portugal

For those people who plan to invest in property in Portugal, close attention should be paid to the sporting facilities on offer. It's the overwhelming reason why people rent in Portugal. Golf is particularly popular. If considering investing look for championship quality courses.

Madeira

Madeira has many charms and attracts a slightly different crowd. It has fertile volcanic soil, good all-year-round weather and has not been spoilt by development. The island has not really been popular with second-homers although this has now changed with increased development on the island which aims to change the landscape whilst retaining the beauty. Well worth a look. The process of buying is the same as mainland Portugal and the rental opportunities are certainly there although again have to be well researched.

*

Useful Information

Estate agents

Hamptons International (offices in various parts of Portugal)

e-mail international@hamptons-int.com

www.aplaceinthesun.com/portugal

www.algarvepropertyguide.com

www.zoopla.co.uk/overseas/property/portugal

www.rightmove.co.uk/overseas-property/Portugal-guide.html

www.aplaceinthesun.com/portugal

Lawyers

https://www.bestlawyers.com/portugal/real-estate-law

https://www.portugalproperty.

Portuguese Embassy London

11 Belgrave Square

London SW1X 3HR

020 7235 5331

www.portugal.embassyhomepage.com

Portuguese National Tourist Office

020 7201 6666

****

Chapter 5

Buying in Italy

Italy is a beautiful country with everything to offer. The countryside is magical, especially around the Tuscan hills and the architecture, art, music and general culture cause many people to fall in love with the country and never come back.

Italy is the home of the Romans, the Renaissance, Catholicism and much great art and wonderful cities and buildings. Italy has been home to many expatriate poets and historians plus writers. Robert Browning and Elizabeth Barrett, Keats and Shelley and Harold Acton.

Many Italian cities have been allowed to remain intact and have thus preserved their ancient charm. Generally speaking, people who move to Italy are those who have fallen in love with the place and want to spend the rest of their live there. Nowhere else will do. Unlike France and Spain, Italy is most definitely not associated with lager louts and mass tourism. There are resorts but even these are more mellow and laid back than their other European counterparts.

Nowhere in Italy guarantees winter warmth. It is not a country where you would go for the climate. Winters can be very cold indeed. However, the sun shines in spring and summer and typical summer temperatures are: Rome 24.1; Milan 22.8; Naples 23.5; Venice 22.5; Pescara 22.9. In winter these temperatures can plummet. Also, many parts of the country are prone to earthquakes, flooding and, in the winter, dense fog. The summer sees droughts, which is a price to pay for the hot weather

Most experts advise renting a place in Italy before deciding where and whether to buy. Do research to see which place suits the best. There is a thriving holiday rental market and they are easy to obtain.

One book that anyone should read before contemplating a move to Italy is Barry Unsworth's *After Hannibal*. This book paints a realistic picture of life in Italy after moving there and is perhaps better than many guide books at painting a vivid and realistic picture of life in Italy for the foreigner.

There are many problems which are encountered by would-be second homers in Italy. For example, in Tuscany stories are legion of estates and houses not being what they seem, particularly in relation to what is for sale, and planning irregularities and so on. As with all other countries, when buying outside of your own land be very careful and have some understanding of the legal system.

Although there is no shortage of properties available in Tuscany, for example, many are not offered for sale on the open market. People with a high net worth (lots of money!) can do complicated private deals with landowners. However, and Italy is characterised by this, picking your way through the tax, legal, local council, planning and ownership issues is not for the ordinary buyer or person of ordinary means. Bureaucracy in Italy is very complex indeed.

It seems that most foreigners who have bought a property in Italy tend to be rich or educated upper-middle class people who don't have to worry too much about money. However, having said that, more and more people are chancing their luck and investigating Italy, drawn by its culture, fine wines, good food and beautiful countryside. There are a number of other reasons, it could be that you are fluent in Italian and have studied Italian art or music. For many reasons you have fallen in love with Italy.

There are a number of factors which need to be considered when thinking of buying a home in Italy. Firstly, Italy is not as close as Spain or France and therefore more difficult to visit on an impulse. Secondly, the process of choosing, buying and renovating a home in Italy is vastly more difficult and expensive than in most other European countries. In spite of this more and more people are choosing Italy. There are many opportunities to find derelict properties. There are over 350 abandoned villages in Italy and some Italian property companies are now working at selling off entire villages for development to foreign buyers. However, in spite of the opportunities Italy does not attract big developers. There are several reasons why. One is that many local councils are still controlled by communists, who do not want high security elitist developments on their farmland. Nor do they want foreigners per se if possible. Essentially, Italy for the Italians not for the fat cats.

Local government in Italy is generally in the hands of thousands of tiny little councils all at constant loggerheads with each other and all with their own ideas on planning and development. Basically, even the biggest construction companies in the world have found that the prospect of building second or holiday homes in Italy is too daunting and they tend to gravitate to countries where the process is easier. There are, at the time of writing, several new developments on the go, in areas that have relaxed restrictions slightly. These are mainly southern Italy, in the Calabria region and tend to be golf, ski and beach apartments. These tend to be in the region of £50,000 plus annual running costs of £1200.

The process of buying in Italy

If you are interested in buying an old house in Italy, a complete wreck, with no roof and very little else, this will cost you around £175,000. There will generally be no basic services at all, no water, electricity or gas and these will need to be installed.

After you have located your property, the next stage will be to get together with a geometra (architect) who will draw up plans for restoration. The geometra is essential as it is necessary to have someone with you who is bilingual and well versed in Italian building terms and culture. The plans have to be approved by the appropriate local council before you proceed. Restoration is expensive and likely to be in the region of £300-£350,000, bringing the total cost to about £500,000 which is a lot to pay for a second home. As I said, it must be a labour of love. Don't attempt to carry out the renovation yourself as you will encounter many problems along the way.

Mortgages are easy to obtain from an English lender for an Italian home but also fairly easy to obtain (subject to market conditions in 2019/20) from an Italian Lender. The legal process of purchasing a home in Italy is very similar to that in France. You will need a notary to check the legal agreement. This stage is very important and it is here that most problems are uncovered. You will certainly need the services of a bilingual solicitor who understands the Italian conveyancing system.

Buying a property in Italy is similar to buying in the UK to the extent that there is an Offer and acceptance procedure, which is usually followed by an exchange of contracts: the Preliminary Act ("Compromesso") and the final deed ("Atto/Rogito Notarile") in front of an Italian Notary. The deed is signed, the balance of the money handed over in exchange for the keys. The contract (deed) is subsequently recorded in the Public/Land Registry.

Most Italian properties are freehold, including apartments.

In Italy, since 1989, an Estate Agent (Agente immobiliare) must be registered in the Register of Estate Agents, held at the Chamber of Commerce. Only professional estate agents, who have taken and passed stringent exams on every aspect of property transactions, can become registered. LiguriaHomes director, Matteo Scandolera, is also an Official Property Consultant of the Imperia Court.

Under Italian Law a property has a Legal or Tax value ("Valore Catastale"); this is a value placed on a property by the Government and is generally considerably less than the commercial price of the property (approx from 30 to 50% of the commercial price). It is the figure on which taxes are calculated as reported in the Local Land Registry Office ("Catasto").

Under Italian Law, there is no penalty fee if you decide to pay the entire mortgage amount, before the original end.

Step by Step Guide
1. Offer to Purchase ("Offerta")

The first step is formalising the Offer to the vendor, through the estate agent as an intermediary. The offer is then placed in writing (in Italian and in English) and you will normally have to pay a deposit on the property (10,000 - 20,000 EUR). If the offer is accepted, this deposit paid is defined as "Caparra Confirmatoria". This transaction – Caparra Confirmatoria – is legally binding. Should either party wish to withdraw from the sale, the other party can either force the sale or claim damages and ask for the return of the down payment. Should the vendor default, you may get double the fee you have paid.

2. Preliminary Contract ("Compromesso" or "Contratto preliminare")

Once the seller accepts the offer, the parties have a binding contract, which is then formalised with the execution of the Preliminary Act (normally from 1 to 3 months after the Offer), a formal agreement according to which the parties undertake to buy and sell the property and agree on the terms and conditions of the sale. This is the most important step during the process. It will contain the details of the sale including the purchase price; the completion date and all the obligations for the vendor and the buyer. It will also contain a full description of the property with all related information such as cadastral details and any planning permission obtained. On signing the "Compromesso", the buyer pays normally between 10% and 20% as deposit ("Caparra Confirmatoria") on the purchase price. At this stage you have to pay the Commission Fee ("Provvigione") to the estate agent.

3. Final Deed of Sale ("Rogito" or "Atto Notarile")

The transfer of the property takes place with the execution of a deed of sale in front of a Notary. The Notary ("Notaio") is the only professional entitled to transfer legal title to properties in Italy. Although the notary is selected and paid by the buyer, he is an independent public officer/professional charged with the duty of drafting the purchase deed finalizing the sale, ensuring that title passes legally between the parties, verifying the necessary legal documentation and registration in the Local Land Register and at the "Conservatoria dei Registri Immobiliari". It is a very important stage and it is necessary for you to understand the details of the contract. That is the reason why we suggest to appoint an english spoken Notary, for ensuring that everything is clear and that you understand all the terms and conditions. A bank account is recommended to make the purchase payment at completion.

Post completion formalities

Once the purchase has been completed in the Notary' office, the foreign buyer will mainly be interested in obtaining a certified copy of the Purchase Deed, as duly lodged with the authorities by the Italian Notary appointed. A copy of the Purchase Deed ("Rogito") is usually available for collection within 2 - 3 months from the date of completion. LiguriaHomes will collect it for you. Where the property is in a block of flats, to inform the condominium manager ("Amministratore del condominio") of the transfer of the flat to the foreign buyer.

Finally, it will be necessary to arrange for new contracts ("Volturazione delle utenze") with the main utilities (power, water, gas, telephone, etc.

Taxes and costs

Taxes on purchase are as follows:

Registration tax/stamp duty ("Imposta di Registro") is paid, in a simplified term, on the governments valuation of the property, the "Valore catastale". If you are buying the property as a holiday home, stamp duty will be 9% of this government valuation. If however you wish to move to Italy and apply for residency ("Prima casa") within 18 months of the closure, then the stamp duty becomes 2% (4% in case of new construction). It is paid at the time of completion, to the Notary.

Three other small taxes (land registration, cadastral and mortgage), in the region of € 50 each are to be paid as a one-off at the time of completion, to the Notary.

The tax to be paid once a property is bought is:

- IMU/TASI property tax ("Imposta Muncipale sugli Immobili") is a local council tax of between 0.7% - 1% of the cadastral value of the property. The actual rate is decided by the local authority on an annual basis and is paid in two installments in June and December. The main residence ("Prima Casa") is not subject to any property tax.

A person not resident in Italy has to make an annual declaration to the Italian tax authorities for any income in relation to activities in Italy (an example of this will be the income derived from letting the Italian property). It is possible to off -set certain expenses against that income – repairs, management expenses, local taxes etc. This income also has to be declared in the country of residence with a double taxation agreement preventing paying twice.

For holiday homes, if the owner sells within 5 years this incurs a charge of 20% Capital Gain on the gain between the buying price and the selling price.

Renting a property out in Italy

There is a high demand for rental property in Italy. The rentals are mainly restored farmhouses, rather than new villas and apartments. The summer rental market for Tuscan farmhouses is huge, because of the general beauty of the area.

Settling in Italy

If you are a citizen of a EU state then there should be no problems concerning residency. It is vital, if you intend to settle permanently, that you take advice from your own tax office concerning taxes and how much you will be liable for in which country. Italy follows broadly the same pattern as Spain and France regarding health care, social security benefits and tax. The cost of living is a lot lower than the UK, the health system is good and the lifestyle generally is more relaxed.

*

Useful Information

Property for sale in Italy

www.rightmove.co.uk/*overseas*-property/*in-Italy.html*

www.casatravella.com

www.italianhousesforsale.com

www.aplaceinthesun.com/italy/hot-properties/italy-hot-beach-properties

Homes in Tuscany

L'Architrave

Tel: +39 0187 475543larchitrave.com

Umbria

https://rightmove.co.uk/overseas-property-for-sale/Umbria.

https://www.immobiliareitaliano.com/location/umbria

Venice

www.venicesothebysrealty.com/buyers

www.primelocation.com/*overseas*/property/*italy*/*veneto*/venice

Lawyers

www.studiolegalemetta.com/en/practice-areas/italian-real-estate

****

Chapter 6

Buying in Greece

As the world knows, Greece has been very hard hit by the world-wide recession and the problems inherent within the European Union. This had a knock on effect on tourism and house buying generally but is now in the process of recovery. Those seeking to buy in Greece will find the prices cheaper than they were before but on the climb.

Notwithstanding this, Greece is a very popular resort for the British and was, along with Spain, one of the first to welcome package holidaymakers. Much of the economy of Greece is based on tourism. It is easy to get to Greece, because of the proliferation of budget airlines, and there are still a lot of Britons wanting to buy holiday homes in the country, in spite of the difficult economic climate

The weather, although hot, is affected by the fact that Greece is in the Northern hemisphere, which means that it can be cold in the winter and spring. Familiar enough territory for UK citizens!

In Greece, there are two distinct types of property for second-homers. There are the older homes situated in villages, usually in need of renovation and the new developments which are springing up all over Greece. The problem with the older homes is that, although they are initially cheap to buy, the renovation can cost a lot of money. Although a newer property may cost more the advantage is that once a person has moved in there are no further costs. Island locations tend to be more expensive than the mainland and island prices are often inflated.

The process of buying in Greece

The cost of a property in Greece is relatively cheap, when compared to the UK. However, as with Italy, the on-costs are high. The purchase of a property in Greece follows, broadly, that of Spain and Portugal, where a notary is needed to make sure that all the papers are in order and there are no problems with the sale.

If you buy an old house in Greece, the first thing to ascertain is exactly who the property belongs to. If it belongs to more than one family member, as is so often the case then you will need to contact all those individual members and ask their permission to purchase the property. A lawyer, well versed in Greek property matters, will need to be instructed.

You will need to obtain a Greek tax number (known in Greece as an AFM-Arithmos Forologikou Mitroou) from the local tax office to satisfy the Greek tax authorities that you do not owe any tax. In addition, as with buying property in many foreign countries it is essential that you have a Greek bank account, which must always be in credit.

As a general rule, Europeans can purchase real estate anywhere in Greece. Foreign nationals from European countries have to obtain prior approval from the local prefecture if they wish to purchase in some defined areas such as Crete and Rhodes. Foreign nationals from non-EU countries have to obtain permission from the Greek Ministry of Defence which usually takes longer. Bear this in mind post-BREXIT!

One major problem with buying property in Greece is that there is no national land registry, as there is in the UK. To acquire a title to a property, a number of steps have to be followed:

- The vendor must provide copies of the title. It is up to the vendor to chase for these, and vitally important.
- The purchaser must then instruct a lawyer to search the titles.
- The purchaser or vendor must approach a public notary who will work with the lawyers to draft the contract deed.

Once the contract deed is signed, filed at the notary's office and transferred at the Registry of Mortgages, the document becomes the official title of the property. The purchaser's lawyers must ensure that all property taxes have been paid and if the building is new or being purchased off-plan that the necessary planning permission has been obtained.

Greek Mortgages
Benefits of a Greek property mortgage
If you are moving permanently to Greece and will be receiving your income in Euros, a Greek mortgage might be a good choice.

This is because having your income and your mortgage payments in the same currency prevents you being affected by movements in the rate of exchange.

If you are buying a second home in Greece, getting a Greek mortgage means that your repayments on the property won ' t be tied to your UK property, as they would be if, for example, you has remortgaged your UK property in order to buy the Greek property. Keeping these elements separate may be the right choice for your circumstances, so that if you have repayment difficulties it is only your second home that is at risk.

Drawbacks of a Greek Property Mortgage

Although on the face of things the process of getting a mortgage in Greece looks similar to the mortgage process in the UK, the reality can often prove different to what you might be used to in Britain. This is because the legal and administration processes in Greece are known for sometimes being little slower and more bureaucratic than in many other European countries. If you want to buy a Greek property off-plan, or you want to build your own home in Greece, you could also face difficulties. This is due to the fact that most Greek mortgage lenders will only allow you to access your mortgage funds once a property has been completed. In the UK you can often access money as the property building process progresses, but this is not usually the case with Greek property. This means that you will usually have to find another way to finance your building project.

General

Greece has not been subject to the same level of unsightly development as, for example, Spain, and the market is a lot more fragmented. Most new properties built in Greece are in smaller complexes or individual units. However, as with everywhere else, do your homework and negotiate with agents and sellers.

There are a number of useful websites concerning purchase of Greek properties and also settling in Greece, at the end of this chapter.

The buyer of property has to pay property transfer taxes before the final contract is concluded. These usually amount to between 7-11% depending on factors such as where the property is located in a region as well as the purchase price. Real estate purchase contracts can only be concluded before a public notary. After the final contract is executed the property must be registered at the local land registry. According to Greek law, the sale of the property is only officially concluded once the property is registered. Overall, the costs of buying will be:

- The property transfer tax
- The public notary fees
- The lawyers fees
- The Land Registry fees
- The estate agents fees

Like the UK, money laundering regulations are in place in Greece and the buyer will need to justify funds and demonstrate where the money came from before being able to proceed.

*

Useful Information

Greek Embassy for general advice

www.greekembassy.org.uk

Buying a property in Greece-General advice including legal advice

www.propertyguides.com/greece/buying

/www.globalpropertyguide.com/Europe/Greece/Buying-Guide

www.apropertyingreece.com

www.fairmortgages.co.uk/mortgages-for-greek-property

www. propertygreece.com/property-for-sale-in-greece/regions-in-greece/

www.rightmove.co.uk/*overseas*-property/in-greece.*html*

ttps://www.green-acres.gr/property-for-sale/peloponnese

Information on Rhodes

placeinthesun.com/property/Greece/Aegean_islands/Rhodes

General

www.aegean-blue.com

www.hellenic-homes.com

Crete

www.europa-crete.com

www.creteproperty.co.uk

****

Chapter 7

Buying in Cyprus

Cyprus has become more and more popular over the last decade or so and more and more Britons are buying up holiday homes or retiring permanently.

Cyprus became a British Crown Colony in 1925 and gained its independence in 1960. Fighting ensued, although now it has been peaceful for a long time and the Island is partitioned, Greek (south) and Turkish Cypriot (north). The division has not really affected tourism or the economy and there is development going on in the Greek sector attracting second homers and retirees.

As incomers are not allowed to earn money in Cyprus, anybody who settles there must satisfy the authorities that they can support themselves. In May 2004, Cyprus joined the EU which brings it in line with other EU countries. On its accession to the EU, Cyprus revised many of its laws that placed restrictions on property investments by citizens of other EU states.

However, it has to be said, be very careful when purchasing a property in Cyprus and make sure you have a good lawyer to avoid any pitfalls.

Buying and selling property in Cyprus

Cypriots & E.U citizens living in Cyprus

Under Cyprus Law, Cypriots or persons of Cypriot origin as well as E.U citizens who have their permanent residence in Cyprus are allowed to acquire any property without any restrictions.

The residential status is ascertained by the District offices and is obtained when a person resides in Cyprus for a total period of 185 days per year or more.

E.U citizens not permanently living in Cyprus & Non E.U citizens

Non-EU citizens are given permission to buy only one apartment or one house or a building plot or land. In the case of EU citizens the property size can be unlimited and in the case of non-E.U citizens it can be up to 4,014 square meters (the equivalent of three donums)

E.U citizens are treated as equal to Cypriot citizens, regardless of their residential status. (Keep an eye out for changes in status following BREXIT).

After the permission has been obtained (see point 3 below) and the property has been registered in the name of the purchaser, there are no other restrictions for foreigners who are the owners of immovable property in Cyprus. They may sell or dispose of the property as they wish. The foreigner owner of an immovable property can sell it and buy another and as any bona fide repeat purchaser will be granted a subsequent permit.

Making an offer

Buying a property in Cyprus is very similar to buying property in the UK. You make an offer and if it is accepted, it is normal to give a nominal deposit (between €1,000 and €5,000) to reserve the property, bind the owner, have the property taken off the market and secure it at that day's price. This in Cyprus, unlike the UK, is legally binding and so "gazumping" does not exist. Contracts are consequently drawn up and this process takes only a few days. Upon signing of the contract, the buyer must pay at least 20%-30% of the value of the property. The remaining sum is paid according to the terms agreed with the seller. Usually for new off-plan properties the payment of includes periodic installments until delivery. If is a resale property the balance is paid in one single payment at the same day when the title deed is transferred on the purchasers name and the purchaser takes possession at the same time.

Acquisition of real estate property in Cyprus includes::

- Transfer of title deed
- Long lease for periods of more than 33 years
- The acquisition of shares in a company that owns immovable property, if such acquisition results in the company becoming controlled by foreigners
- The establishment of a trust or any type of set-up, which is connected with the ownership of real estate, for the benefit of a foreigner, including tax benefits

Specific performance-safeguards for the buyer

Specific Performance Law safeguards a purchaser of immovable property from a transaction between a seller and a purchaser, especially when the purchaser is not allowed to immediately transfer the acquired property onto his/her name even though payment of the consideration has been effected.

According to the provisions of Specific Performance Law, the purchaser of immovable property may secure the transfer of the acquired property onto his/her name by depositing a duly signed and stamped copy of the contract at the Land Registry, within two (2) months from the signing of the contract.

By depositing the contract in the Land Registry, the purchaser prevents the owner from transferring the property elsewhere or changing it, for as long as the contract is valid and legally effective. No burdens, charges or encumbrances can affect the right of specific performance after the contract has been deposited with the Land Registry.

Depositing a copy of the contract to the Land Registry gives the purchaser the right to seek "specific performance" of the terms and conditions of the contract and thus to register the property onto the purchaser's name, even though the owner may not be willing to accommodate such procedures.

Fees, charges and property taxes
Transfer fees

The transfer of immovable property into a purchaser's name can be effected once permission to acquire the property has been granted from the Council of Ministers/Pertinent Authority (where that is necessary – see point 3 above).When registering the property under his/her name at the District Land Office, the purchaser will be liable to pay the following transfer fees, calculated according to the property's market value at the time of signing of the contracts:

Stamp duty

Unless otherwise stipulated in the contract, the purchaser is liable for the payment of stamp duty at the rate of 0.15% of the value of the property up to €170,000 and 0.20% for over €170,000

The contract should be stamped within a period of thirty (30) days from signing. Although the absence of the revenue stamp on a contract does not render it void, the revenue stamp must be paid before depositing the contract to the Land Registry for specific Performance purposes (see point 4 above) The stamp duty plus a fine will be payable when the document is produced to the Land Office for the transfer of ownership of property, to any Government department or to the court. In order to avoid the payment of a fine, which could be substantial, the documents should be stamped within 30 days of their signing.

Immoveable (Towns) property tax

The registered owner of immovable property is also subject to minor taxation under other laws, such as municipal or village regulations. These taxes are calculated according to the area and the size of the property and cover sewerage, refuse collection, street lights. The charges range in total from €80 to €170 per annum.

Capital Gains tax

Capital Gains tax is levied at the rate of 20% on gains arising from the disposal of immovable property or the disposal of shares of companies the assets of which consist mainly on immovable property.

As a general rule, the gain is calculated as the difference between the sales proceeds and the original cost of the property. Interest on payments paid for the acquisition, additions to the property and inflation rate, as published yearly by the Government, are deducted form fees.

Capital gains tax as a whole has minimal effect, since the appreciation of values, coupled with the following allowances and inflation, tend to leave little excess.

Individuals are entitled to the following lifetime allowances on Capital Gains Tax:

- The first €17,086.00 of gains arising from the disposal of any property are exempted.
- The first €25,629.02 of gains arising from the disposal of agricultural land by the farmer are exempted (subject to certain conditions).
- The first €85,430.10 of gains arising from the disposal of a house used by the owner for his/her own habitation are exempted (subject to certain conditions).

The above allowances are not available separately and an individual claiming a combination of the above allowances is only allowed a maximum lifetime allowance of € 85,430.10

Cyprus residents and companies registered in Cyprus are subject to Capital Gains Tax when disposing their property, wherever it is, in Cyprus or overseas. However, under certain conditions, Capital Gains Tax can be reduced significantly if the purchase of the immovable property is effected through a Cyprus registered company.

The following categories of immovable property disposals are exempted from the Capital Gains Tax:

1. Transfers by reason of death
2. Gifts between relatives up to third degree of kindred
3. Gifts to limited liability companies when, at the time of transfer and for a period of five years following the transfer, all the shareholders of the company are members of the family of the donor
4. Gifts by family companies to their members, but only in cases where the property transferred, was obtained by the company as a gift
5. Exchanges of immovable properties
6. Compulsory acquisitions
7. Gifts to charitable institutions
8. Gifts to charitable institutions or the Republic of Cyprus

Communal expenses

Communal expenses are usually payable monthly or quarterly, in advance, and vary from development to development depending on the area and type of the property. They cover an immovable property's owner share of the cost of cleaning and maintaining common areas and gardens, communal swimming pool expenses, electricity in common areas, management fees and repairs.

At this point in time, about 90% of foreign buyers in Cyprus are British, with many settling permanently on the island. The legal and real estate systems are based on the British model so a degree of familiarity will be present.

As a destination to retire, Cyprus has a lot to offer. It has a warm year round climate and is very hot in the summer. The cost of living is slightly lower than the UK and it is possible to live off an income of around £8,000 a year, although this means being very frugal. Since 2007, the cost of living in Cyprus has risen significantly and you will need to do your research before deciding to settle there. Another attraction of the island is that there are a lot of sports on offer.

There are currently three markets of incomers in Cyprus, those seeking a holiday home, those seeking a retirement home and those seeking a second home, who will spend longer on the island than a holiday homer but are not yet ready to retire. English is the widely adopted second language so, unlike say Greece, language will not be a problem.

If you are interested in permanent retirement in Cyprus, then you must obtain an immigration permit issued by the

Minister of the Interior of the Republic of Cyprus. Tax would normally be paid in the UK. Ownership of homes is limited to one per foreign alien so it is not possible to build up a string of properties for investment purposes. Mortgages are available on properties in Cyprus subject to the usual paperwork.

Renting out a property in Cyprus

Although it used to be the case that foreigners could not create a business renting out properties in Cyprus, the law has now changed, restrictions relaxed and non-residents are allowed to rent out properties, as long as they abide by the tax laws. There are tight restrictions on the number of properties that a foreigner can own. The square metreage mentioned earlier applies to pure investors although you can now set up a business in Cyprus to hold properties. As with all other countries, location, location, location applies. The closer to the sea, the better the amenities the better the rental market.

Investment generally

There has been a lot of development going on in Cyprus aimed at the investor. Investors have usually been advised to steer clear of Northern Cyprus, although the area is now being heavily marketed and the systems in this part of Cyprus are being refined. A relatively recent case, involving a retired couple David and Linda Horams highlighted the problems inherent when buying property in Northern Cyprus. They purchased a piece of land in Northern Cyprus in 2003 and soon after completing the development of the land into a luxury retirement home they were sued by a Mr Apostolides, a Greek Cypriot who maintained that he had owned the land when Turkish forces invaded in 1974. When Mr Apostolides managed to cross south to north in 2004, he found the house on his land. He fought the case and eventually lost, being left with a huge legal bill. The case has paved the way for other people to buy in the North as it lifts, somewhat, the burden of buying/developing a home only to find that you can lose it. This does not remove the possibility that you may be challenged at any time.

Overall, the Greek side of the Island is the safer bet, and the most familiar in terms of fellow Britons to buy a home. You can, if you wish, and if your passport has at least six months to run, enter Northern Cyprus. Nationalities from outside the EU will probably need a visa to enter Northern Cyprus. The currency is the same as Turkey, the Turkish Lira.

*

Useful Information

Southern Cyprus

Cyprus Property Services

Mercia House

3 Brickhill Close

Blunham

Beds MK44 3NF

www.paphosproperty.com

Cyprus Property Direct Limited

www.cyprospropertydirect.com

Cyprus Tourist Board

visitcyprus.com

Legal Advice

www.aplaceinthesun.com/cyprus/advice/legal/buying-process

www.property-abroad.com/cyprus/lawyers-solicitors

Northern Cyprus

Unwin Estate Agents

www.unwinestates.com

Landmark Estate Agency

http://www.north-cyprus-properties-landmark.com/

****

Chapter 8

Buying in Malta and Gibraltar

Malta

Malta is a fascinating island with a rich but bloody history. This is mainly because of its strategic position in the centre of the Mediterranean. It was a British colony for 150 years and was for a long time a naval base. The author was himself based in Malta in 1970, during the heyday, before the Church and state joined forces to change matters. Nowadays, the old sleazy side of Malta, mainly in Valletta, has been cleaned up and the armed forces long gone.

Every year, up to 2 million tourists visit this former British colony. It is very 'British' in its feel and also has a host of other influences, Moorish, Spanish and French. It is also a very popular second home location for many people.

Malta has a lot to offer those who are seeking a second home. It is very easy to buy a property if you are a foreign national, with few restrictions. Cost of living and personal taxation is low and the health service, which has reciprocal agreements with the UK is regarded as good. There are many sports, both on mainland Malta and also on Gozo which is a nearby Island. Crime is almost non-existent, in large measure to do with the strength of family ties and the influence of the church. The weather is good and the main language is English, although there is an official Maltese language.

Where to buy

Character homes in secluded, community minded villages set in Naxxar, Rabat and Lija are popular and attract retirees, expat buyers and young families. There have been a number of new developments coming on stream such as the traditionally styled Madliena Village in historic Gharghur and Ta Monita in Marsacala. prices start in the region of £130,000 for a one bed apartment.

The process of buying a property in Malta

The process of buying a property is clear-cut in Malta Foreign investors can own one property. The exception to the rule is if you reside in Malta on a permanent basis for five years, then you can purchase additional stand-alone property. Foreign nationals who are from non-EU countries can also buy property in Malta, but they should get a permit called the Acquisition of Immovable Property (AIP) Permit from Malta's Ministry of Finance. Getting this permit may take 3 months, at least. There will be a cost for estate agents, higher than in the UK. They   will charge 5% plus VAT if the sale is an open purchase (with more than one agent) and 3.5% plus VAT if with one agent. You will need to use a notary (your solicitor), as below.

Once you have located your desired home then an offer is made, accepted and a preliminary agreement, known as a 'convenue (which is a binding contract) is signed between the vendor and purchaser. Once this is signed a 10% deposit is lodged with the notary public who acts as a stakeholder. As with purchases in the UK, if the buyer pulls out the deposit is lost and given to the purchaser. Once the agreement has been signed the notary will carry out necessary searches and deal with all applications etc. The buyer pays approximately 0.1-0.5% of purchase price for these searches. When this is complete then a deed of sale is drawn up by the purchaser's notary and at this stage the balance of all payments will be paid.

The general expense involved in a purchase of a property in Malta will be 3.5% on properties up to 150,000 Euros 5% duty on properties above that amount. Stamp duty is payable in two instalments 1% midway through the process and 4% on completion, notary fees of around 1% of purchase price, fees for searches and registration plus a Ministry of Finance fee. The seller will pay stamp duty on the purchase price. If the property is to be the buyers main residence then they would be charged 3.5% plus VAT on the first 150,000 euros of the purchase price then 5% on the rest.

Tax on sale/Capital gains tax

In Malta, Capital Gains Tax is actually a transaction cost and not a tax on capital gains. Capital Gains Tax is generally levied at a flat rate of 12% on the transfer value or the selling price. Only brokerage fees can be deducted from the selling price. During the sale, a provisional tax equal to 12% of the selling price must be paid to the notary public who will then pass it on to the Inland Revenue as payment of the tax liability.

If the seller has inherited the property before 25 January 1992, capital gains tax is levied at a flat rate of 7%. If the seller is not involved in property trading, capital gains tax may be levied at a final withholding tax rate of 5% on properties that were sold within five years of acquisition. If the seller has acquired the property prior to 01 January 2004, capital gains tax is levied at a final withholding tax rate of 10%.

Capital Gains Tax Exemption

Should an EU Citizen whilst being a permanent resident of Malta use a property as his/her primary residence for at least 3 consecutive years, he/she would not be liable to pay Capital Gains Tax when selling such property after the said 3 year period and provided that it is sold within 12 months of vacating the property.

General

Non-Maltese purchasers, as elsewhere, must satisfy the Ministry of Finance that adequate funds are available to buy the property and the property that has been purchased is for sole or family use only.

If the property has been purchased as an investment to let out permission must be gained to rent out to third parties. This is usually a formality. There is a thriving rental industry and people are actively encouraged to rent out their properties.

As stated, generally foreign nationals are allowed to buy only one property in Malta. If a person wishes to buy a second property then the first one must be sold. There are all sorts of properties for sale, from new apartments (sadly parts of Malta have succumbed to over development and are unattractive) to town houses and villas. Non-Maltese may be refused permission to buy a property of historic interest.

Mortgages are easily obtainable to non-Maltese and capital gains tax is levied on sale. Malta's membership of the EU has done a lot to ease restrictions on real estate purchase by foreigners. Property prices can vary from anywhere between £80,000 and £170,000.

As mentioned, EU membership has had a major impact on the Maltese property market. An increasing number of EU citizens, in the main British, are looking to relocate to Malta. The weather is good and the cost of living is low although like everywhere it is getting more expensive. (Readers should note that the situation will change once the UK has exited out of the EU).

Financially there are incentives to move to Malta. The 1988 Residence Scheme entitled people to remain in Malta with the freedom to come and go as they please. Alternatively, incomers can obtain an extended tourist permit which enables them to stay longer than three months allowed to an ordinary tourist. The government must be satisfied that the person applying has enough income and capital to finance their stay and not become a burden on the state.

Income tax is levied at a rate of 0-35%. There is no inheritance tax in Malta although there is a 5% transfer tax on real estate at the time of death. In the case of a spouse dying this amount is levied on half the value of the property.

No foreigner is allowed to engage in business in Malta unless authorised by the Maltese Government. There are also restrictions on the work that a foreigner is allowed to do. Malta has signed tax treaties with most countries in Western Europe and also Canada and Australia. These agreements allow Maltese residents to claim back tax from the country from where the income originates, and obtain double taxation relief from Malta. Pets can be imported into Malta subject to restrictions on rabies and quarantine.

There is a thriving rentals market in Malta and there are no restrictions to letting property to foreigners.

Gibraltar

Gibraltar is another place which has a very British feel to it. You can access Gibraltar by walking across a causeway from the Southern tip of Spain and you will walk into a world of red telephone boxes, British Bobbies and English pubs. Basically, Gibraltar is a time warp, a British colony. Like Malta, because of its strategic location Gibraltar has had a difficult military history. The interior is rather dreary and the only real attraction, apart from military relics, are the Apes.

Gibraltar is a tax haven and has been targeted by property developers and there is more and more property for sale on the island. The conveyancing system is similar to Britain. The overall advantages to buying in Gibraltar are tax, weather, Britishness (if that is what is wanted) and its proximity to Spain.

*

Useful Information

The websites below offer general advice on buying, selling and renting property in Malta and Gibralter. There are many more sites other than those listed.

Malta

www.propertymaltadirect.com

www.propertylinemalta.com

www.property-abroad.com/malta/buyers-guide

www.perry.com.mt/en/overseas-buyers-guide

www.maltahomes.net/buying-advice.

Gibraltar

propertygibraltar.com/forsale

www.propertyworld.gi/buying.htm

www.rightmove.co.uk/overseas-property/in-Gibraltar

www.expatfocus.com/destinations/gibraltar/guide/buying-property

www.primelocation.com/overseas/property/gibraltar

Chapter 9

The United States of America and Canada

Prior to the credit crunch in 2008, which engulfed America (and the rest of the world), and decimated its property market, there was a property boom right across the states. Florida was the main destination for property buyers, with Disneyworld on the doorstep and also the dozens of other theme parks. It is likely to remain a popular destination and, although the property market has slowed right down, there are now signs that it is picking up.

Florida property

For those who wish to buy, Florida has much to offer second-homers, retirees and families with children. There are the many Disney attractions and all the other theme parks, such as Universal. There is coast and intra-coastal waterways and many lakes (watch out for the crocs). There is sport in abundance.

The developed parts of the coast in Florida tend to be very expensive indeed, in particular Miami and development is restricted. Prices here tend to be stable, unaffected by the downturn. Most of the new developments tend to be inland.

The obvious difference between buying a second home in the USA and buying in Europe or nearby is the distance and expense of getting there. This is an important factor as travel can be very expensive particularly if you are hauling a family across the pond.

Most of the property companies are now working overtime plugging the benefits of buying a property in Florida. There is a buoyant rental market but make sure that what you buy is close to the amusements and has a pool.

If you go to any property fair in the UK, or elsewhere in Europe you will discover that all the US homes being expensively marketed are the new Florida developments However, be careful. Prices have dropped and there are bargains to be had and it might be preferable to take a trip over there. Many agents are now running property tours and are showing apartments and houses that are significantly reduced in price.

One thing that would-be buyers have to watch out for is the fact that Florida has zoning laws which will forbid certain areas from renting out properties for vacation lets. If you are buying a property to rent out you must buy a home that is 'zoned' for rental. For example in a development of 200 houses only half might be zoned for vacation use. In the residential areas you are only allowed yearly rentals and the vacation homes cannot be used as main homes but only for short-term rentals of a week or two at a time.

Experts say that if you intend to buy in Miami then it is better to buy an apartment as opposed to a house. It is not a good idea to leave a house unattended for any length of time, unless you are within a gated complex and there are maintenance staff on hand. This is not so much to do with crime but to do with the termites, cockroaches and other insects that can do damage to your house in a tropical climate.

The process of buying a property in the USA

Anybody interested in buying an apartment anywhere in the USA, will usually be vetted very closely by the residents committee of a particular development. The residents association want to ensure that any incomers fit in with the ethos of a development and are financially sound. If the residents association does not like you and doesn't want you then you will not be allowed to purchase.

As a resident of the UK, you can buy an apartment for cash or through a mortgage. There are two types of apartments in the USA, co-ops or condominiums. If you buy a co-op you are allocated a percentage share. With condominiums you buy a specific unit. Mortgage companies favour condominiums. As a general guideline you will have to put down a 30% deposit to secure a co-op but only 5-10% for a condominium, if buying through a mortgage.

If you intend to make an offer on a property-whether or not that offer is accepted, you put down around £1,000 deposit. This is put into an escrow account and untouched until the deal proceeds. If it falls through the money is returned to you in full. This deposit is required to secure a valid contract and to move the deal forward to the next stage.

The next stage involves an inspection, or survey of the property. If buying on a mortgage, much the same as anywhere else, the lender will insist on this. If paying cash it is equally advisable.

When these initial stages are completed you are ready to move to the next stage which is to put down a 10% deposit. Completion is called closure and closure takes between three and six weeks if there are no complications. As usual there are on costs associated with purchasing a property in the USA. For a buyer there is a tax of between $1-$4 per $1,000 of purchase price. This is dependant on where you buy and is a federal tax, similar to stamp duty, paid by the buyer. The seller will also pay a similar tax, at a higher rate.

There is the title insurance policy, to ensure that the title is free of any encumbrances and also debts. If buying on a mortgage this is compulsory, if paying cash voluntary. The policy will cost around $1,500 and will guarantee you the title should it be challenged after purchase. It is also necessary, as elsewhere, to carry out a title search. The attorneys fees will be around $500-700. As with apartments everywhere there will also be a service charge and, for all US property, property taxes levied on the supposed value of the property. When buying any apartment anywhere in the USA, look very carefully at what you are buying.

The more services that you get the more service charges you will pay.

Financing

It is possible to obtain financing for a purchase by a foreign buyer. However, foreigners are more likely to pay higher interest rates and be required to make larger down payments (often 40% or more of the purchase price). Again, this is because of the relative risk of a foreign buyer, who may be impossible to serve with legal process and whose assets may be untouchable, versus a domestic buyer who will be easier to track down and who is subject to the state and national laws should a default occur.

Investment and Immigration into the USA

Newcomers can buy business in Florida, for example, as long as they have at least $125,000 cash invested (but check current figures in 2019) in the business and the business is an active concern. In this case and for these people, an E2 Treaty Investor Visa, valid for five years, can be obtained. There is a high cost, around $5,000 for such a visa. The American Embassy can give you details (see useful websites at the back of the book). Also, take note that since the era of Donald Trump it is always advisable to carefully check what is needed to settle and start a business.

Pure investment into undeveloped real estate, for example, is not allowed. In Florida (although other US states may be different) there is no state income tax as such, but you may be required to pay federal taxes. However, anyone who receives income from renting property or by any other means is required to file a tax return by 1st April each year. If you intend to rent out your property in the USA then it is essential that you receive sound tax advice beforehand. In relation to actual immigration, it is fairly simple to obtain a six month visa if you own a holiday home. Longer visas are available but immigration lawyers are required and the process is costly.

Capital gains, as in most other countries, is payable on your home if and when you sell it.

Generally, it is difficult to retire in Florida for example, unless you are an immediate or close relative of a citizen of the USA. You may also stay if you are a close relative of an alien with a green card.

Investor and priority worker visas are available for those who can either invest a large sum in a US business or have a specialist skill that is needed.

There are no reciprocal health care agreements between the UK and the USA and it is absolutely essential to have private medical insurance. We have all heard of the nightmare stories of going on holiday in the USA and coming back with a leg in plaster and a $100,000 dollar bill for services rendered.

Canada

Reasons for choosing Canada.

Increasing numbers of British people are choosing Canada as the location for their second home, attracted by its spectacular scenery, laid-back lifestyle, political and social stability. Easier travel and increasing coverage by low-cost airlines are also considerations, as is the fact that Canada's international homes market is still young and developers seeking to attract British buyers therefore have to provide good value.

- The Canadian residential property market has performed well in recent years, and is only suffering from the global recession by the economy's association with world markets. Residential property is generally cheaper than in the UK, which, along with historically healthy capital appreciation, makes it an attractive investment for British second home purchasers or those looking to emigrate permanently.

- Canada is said to have weathered the global recession better than almost any other developed economy in the world, the government having put aside money when times were good and there was a budget surplus for 12 years. The problems currently being seen by Canadian companies are almost exclusively as a result of their exposure to global markets. This give property in Canada a real chance of surviving the recession well, despite fact that prices are currently on the slide.

Look for the popular locations.

Down the years, intrepid Britons have immigrated to every part of Canada. For those contemplating the purchase of a holiday home, however, travel time and cost will probably govern the choice of location. These will vary considerably depending on whereabouts in the UK you live. Owing to the comparative ease of travel, British second home purchasers have traditionally favoured eastern Canada. However, the recent introduction of low-cost transatlantic services has led to increased interest in western areas. Purpose-built resorts are also proving popular. We hope this guide provides a place to start. There are many resources to help with further research, including television and radio programs, magazines, the Internet and property exhibitions, as well as estate agents in both the UK and Canada.

- Eastern Canada - Homes in eastern Canada are generally cheaper than comparable ones in the west. Traditionally, Montreal has had the lowest residential property prices of Canada's major urban areas. However, they are now increasing rapidly, so this may be a good place to consider investing. The area has much to offer. Beautiful countryside and excellent sporting facilities, including skiing, are within easy reach. The US is 40 minutes to the south. Boston and New York are six hours' drive away, or an hour by air. There are several daily flights to London, in a flight time of approximately seven hours. Because of its strong rental market, Toronto is also growing in popularity. Rental yields in both Toronto and Montreal have held up well despite the credit crunch.

- Vancouver - British Columbia, Canada's westernmost province, is also one of its most beautiful, with glorious mountains, lakes, rivers and beaches. It has Canada's most temperate climate and some of its friendliest people.

Vancouver, the largest city, is the most expensive area of Canada for residential property. The city, with the neighbouring ski resort of Whistler, is to host the 2010 Winter Olympics, a fact that has to lead to further price increases. Transport links with the UK are improving. There are direct daily services from London to Vancouver (flight time approximately 9.5 hours).

- The Rocky Mountains - Many people visit the Rocky Mountains on holiday and fall in love with this spectacular area. However, property tends to be expensive and, as much of it is situated within national parks, out of bounds to most purchasers. An area worth considering is Canmore in Alberta. Given that it is next to the Banff and Kananaskis national parks, only an hour's drive from Calgary's international airport (flight time to London approximately nine hours) and in a temperate climate zone, it is no surprise that Canmore has doubled its population since it hosted the Winter Olympics in 1988. Prices are relatively low, but increasing. Prices are also rising in Calgary, a young city with a strong first-time buyer market.

- Resorts - Canada is the world's tenth most popular tourist destination but still offers great potential for growth. Recognizing this, the government has invested huge sums in tourism, particularly in the east, which until recently was largely neglected as a holiday destination. Consequently, resort developments are now big business. More and more Britons are seeing the advantages of buying resort properties. Many of them are skiers frustrated by the costs and crowds of European skiing. However, most resorts, even those offering winter sports, are now year-round, with family-oriented attractions. These factors help to extend the rental season and attract a wider range of purchasers. As a bonus, build quality is generally high, maintenance is arranged by a management company and capital appreciation tends to be excellent, particularly in eastern Canada.

Buying a property.

Know the rules and regulations. Regulations on property purchase vary throughout Canada, so it is important to find out about them when you are researching an area. In British Columbia, New Brunswick, Newfoundland, Nova Scotia, Ontario and Quebec, for example, there are no restrictions on foreign ownership, provided you spend less than six months per year in Canada. However, in Banff, which is located within a national park, only businesses and employees of the park can own property, and even they can do so only through renewable 42-year leaseholds.

- Each province has a different limit on the amount and kind of land that can be owned. Unless buying a new property from a developer, potential purchasers are required to register with an estate agent (realtor).

Familiarize yourself with the purchase process. The purchase process in Canada is different from that in the UK and elsewhere, and the practice of gazumping is unknown. As the majority of Canadian realtors cooperate in multiple listings, one realtor can usually access information on all available properties in an area. Once you have chosen a property, you should appoint an independent realtor (or buyer's agent) to represent your interests. In the majority of real estate transactions, the seller pays both the realtors involved. Your agent will draft an Offer to Purchase, which will then be submitted with a deposit, which is refundable should the sale fall through. Once the offer is signed by both vendor and purchaser and any conditions (for example, mortgage approval) are met, the sale can proceed.

Costs of transactions.

Transactions costs in Canada, while varying from province to province, usually comprise between 4.7 and 11 per cent of the property price, making it one of the cheaper places to buy from a fees perspective. A Goods and Services Tax (GST) of 7 per cent and a Provincial Sales Tax (PST) of up to 10 per cent are usually included in the asking price of new homes. Alberta is the only province that does not levy PST.

- In New Brunswick, Newfoundland and Labrador and Nova Scotia, GST is combined with an 8 per cent provincial retail sales tax to form Harmonized Sales Tax (HST) of 15 per cent.
- Subject to certain conditions, GST and HST can be reduced or avoided (see Taxation section). Buying costs vary between

provinces, but purchasers should allow up to £2,000 for legal fees, a survey and insurance. Purchase tax of between 0.5 per cent and 2 per cent of the price is also payable.

Financing a purchase.

When working out how to finance your purchase, consider all the options. Paying cash, if you can afford to do so, is often recommended, but you may not want to tie up a relatively large sum in this way. The other options are remortgaging your UK home or arranging a mortgage on your Canadian property through a Canadian or UK lender. Remortgaging offers the easiest solution. Releasing equity in a UK home means that the second home can be purchased for cash, without the need for another mortgage. However, this may only be feasible for those who own their first home outright.

- Several UK mortgage providers will lend funds of up to 80 per cent of the purchase price for second home purchase over, typically, a 15-year term.

The taxation system.

Canada's tax system - Both the federal and provincial governments impose income taxes, which together make up more than 40 per cent of total tax revenue. Taxes are progressive, the wealthy paying a higher percentage of their income than the less well off. Canada has no Inheritance Tax as such. Inheritance is treated as the disposal of an asset and is therefore subject to Capital Gains Tax, currently 25 per cent.

- A number of other federal, provincial and local taxes are payable by individuals, including sales taxes (see Costs section of Buying a Property) and property taxes. Residential properties are subject to annual local taxes of between 0.5 per cent and 2 per cent of their value.

- Taxation of non-residents - Non-residents pay federal and provincial income tax on Canadian-sourced income. As the UK has a comprehensive double taxation treaty with Canada, taxes paid in Canada may reduce UK liability. GST and HST are charged on new homes purchased for private use. However, in some circumstances – for example, if the owner of a resort property commits it to a rental pool and uses it for 10 per cent of the year or less – a home is classified as commercial property and not subject to tax. Rental income is taxed at 25 per cent, but expenses can be offset against tax.

- A non-resident selling a property in Canada must pay Capital Gains Tax of 25 per cent, levied on a percentage of the profit.

- Passports and visas - To enter Canada as a visitor, a UK national must be in possession of a standard 10-year passport. Visas are not generally necessary, though there are some exceptions. Non-residents can spend up to six months per year in Canada.

- Residency - Permanent resident status gives a non-Canadian the right to live in Canada. Certain residency obligations must be met in order to maintain it. Those desiring permanent residence must apply for landed immigrant status. As this is a complicated process, it is wise to consult a lawyer specializing in immigration.

Mortgages generally in Canada

Generally, banks outside of Canada are unable to lend money on Canadian properties. Canadian institutions, however, are willing to finance non-residents with minimum down-payments of 35% of the purchase price. Canadian financial institutions differ from other international lenders. Typically, mortgages in Canada are term mortgages or alternatively balloon mortgages wherein the mortgage is set for a term and then must be refinanced/renewed at the end of the term. A Canadian mortgage is for 25 years, typically.

*

Useful Information - United States

*www.expatfocus.com/*buying-a-home-in-the-usa-*expat-realtor-advice*

www.rightmove.co.uk/overseas-property/in-USA

www.globalpropertyguide.com/North-America/United-States/Buying-Guide

www.aplaceinthesun.com/usa

www.elitelahomes.com/2011/01/buying-real-estate-in-the-usa-for-non-us-citizen

New England

mainlinenewengland.com

www.luxuryrealestate.com/destinations/new_england

California

www.HomeGain.com

https://www.realtor.com/realestateandhomes-search/Ca

Canada

https://www.aplaceinthesun.com/canada.aspx

www.cic.gc.ca/english/newcomers/after-housing-buy.asp

****

Chapter 11

The Caribbean

Caribbean islands are becoming more and more popular for second homers, with the respective governments encouraging developers to build and people to buy. However, many of the developments are aimed at the well off, with that old chestnut, golf, being promoted heavily.

The Caribbean islands are very diverse, offering a huge cultural and ethnic mix, with art and music, festivals, fishing, cruises and, of course, golf. These can be enjoyed if you have the money to do so. The main point is that the Caribbean is far away from the UK, the weather is superb, but to enjoy it you need money.

Many people who originally emigrated to Britain in the 50's and 60's are now buying retirement homes in their original birthplace. The market for seasonal homes is very big indeed.

During the 1990's the Caribbean changed, there was increased liberalisation and deregulation. For many, it became much more attractive to buy a second home or to engage in pure investment. Most of the islands offer a wide choice of homes from luxury villas, condominiums, villas, mountain farms and beachfront apartments. It is fairly easy to buy a plot of land and develop your own home. It is also fairly easy to rent out your property to holiday-makers, such is the popularity of the islands.

Each island is autonomous and therefore has slightly different methods of purchasing property, financing that purchase and on –costs when buying. A few examples are listed below. As there are so many islands it is not possible to cover them all but two examples are highlighted.

Barbados

Barbados is very popular with holidaymakers and is perhaps the most British of islands. Although there are no restrictions on non-nationals buying a home, it is not possible to arrange finance for the purchase. Anyone intending to buy a property must bring the capital with them and deposit it in the Central Bank of Barbados. The capital can be by mortgage. Mortgages are available for around 50-70% of the property value, and must be approved by an offshore financial institution. Permission from this bank has to be obtained before a non-national can purchase property on the island. The legal costs associated with the purchase amount to around 2% of the purchase price plus VAT. If an agent is employed their fees are about 5% of the purchase price plus VAT at 15%. The vendor, in addition, has to pay a transfer tax of 10%. There is 1% stamp duty

The process of purchasing a property is about three months from start to finish. Homes are easily rentable on Barbados. Tax of between 15-25% is payable on income received. VAT is also payable if the property is let out on a short-term basis, currently at 7%. All properties on Barbados are subject to an annual land tax, depending on size and location.

When selling the property a property land tax of around 7.5% is payable. There is no capital gains tax payable.

The Cayman Islands

The Cayman Islands are not everyone's first idea of a second home, yet are very popular for obvious reasons. They are a well known tax haven and there are virtually no taxes, no property taxes, no income tax, no capital gains tax, no inheritance tax, no taxes at all (almost). It is easy to see why many, many people, some of dubious means, monies of dubious origin, set up home there. There is no restriction of foreign ownership of property, low crime rates and guaranteed good weather (although it does get windy). The main source of income for the island is that of financial services.

The process of buying a property in the Cayman Islands is perhaps one of the simplest anywhere. It is based on the American model, only moves quicker. The system of purchase is known as the Torrens, a mixture of Canadian and American land purchase laws, which is widely used throughout the Caribbean. Unlike Barbados, mortgages are available through local or international banks, and like anywhere else you can borrow if you can repay. The repayment schedule is 10-15 years and the only duty payable on purchase is between 7-9% stamp-duty. There is also a thriving rental market on the islands. Given the size and population of the islands, there are an astonishing number of banks, 533 in total. This makes it, relatively speaking, one of the biggest banking centres in the world. However, the

Cayman Islands are not the only Caribbean tax haven, Bermuda is also tax-free. So what entices people to the Caymans? Essentially, the Caymans are established, as would be expected and there is not the same feeling of racial tensions as can be felt elsewhere in the Caribbean.

Altogether there are 7,000 islands in the Caribbean. They are different but most are now highly regulated and foreign investment is actively encouraged. The laws governing property ownership will vary and, again this is a must, careful research is essential before deciding where to buy. For those unfamiliar with the Caribbean then the most high profile and popular of the islands are where the most purchases take place. These countries are well established and relatively safe when buying a home. If a person chooses to go off the beaten track, as it were, then this is usually because they have met someone who has successfully moved there and can offer advice.

*

Useful Information

The Caribbean

www.caribbeanbuyingguide.com

www.caribbeanlandandproperty.com

www.knightfrank.com/caribbean

www.aplaceinthesun.com/Caribbean/barbados.aspx

www.tropicalconnections.co.uk/buying-property-in-the-caribbean

www.caribbeanandco.com/10-tips-buying-property-caribbean

Chapter 12

The Growth of Eastern Europe

Without a doubt the growth of the European Economic Community and membership of the Community has opened up many countries in terms of property investment over the last decade or so. As increased foreign investment flows into countries so the price of land rises, and so correspondingly does the price of property and rental prices. However, the countries that have joined the EU are very diverse and attract many different types of buyers, whether pure investors or second homers. Some of the markets have been opening up for a while, such as Bulgaria, which has been very heavily hyped and has attracted lots of investors.

There are stories of over development and people losing money in Bulgaria, although this is due more to a lack of investment expertise than anything else. A few years ago people were flocking there, buying all sort of property ranging from whole towns to small farmhouses, going for a song, to seafront apartments. Like everything though, saturation point is reached after a while and people turn to other European destinations, such as Croatia. Each country differs as to legal systems, availability of finance and ease of travel to and fro. Budget airlines are not always available when you want them!

Because the countries are opening up and are relatively new to tourism, opportunities are definitely there. Property buying usually follows tourism. However, where tourism is not yet established there may not be, probably will not be, a rental market, which limits the potential for investment.

Bulgaria

As mentioned above, Bulgaria became the most hyped of all the new European destinations. Everywhere that you looked, there were developers promoting the virtues of the black sea and the ski slopes of Bansko or Pamporavo, which were rapidly developed.

Bulgaria has a lot to offer. It is rich in natural resources, has beautiful beaches, stunning mountains and natural spas and, despite rampant development, still has much to offer. One other advantage of its growth has been the fact that its legal systems are quite well established. Golf courses are also being developed, in a move aimed at drawing golf fanatics away from Spain and Portugal. The spa resorts of Velingrad and Albenia are famous for their mineral waters, and have been so for a very long time.

The capital of Bulgaria, Sofia, is rapidly developing into a modern European city thanks to investment and there is a burgeoning buy-to-let market. Those in the know advise people, investor's, to buy wisely, not to buy too cheaply as it is the facilities on offer that will attract renters.

However, notwithstanding the attractions, the Bulgarian system of property purchase has its anomalies which put off would be investors. It is the case, currently, that you can buy buildings and not land. This makes people nervous. Foreigners are allowed to buy title to buildings, or part of buildings, such as apartments, and the right to build on land belonging to someone else. To get round this, most foreigners form a company, which is allowed in Bulgaria, and they buy the land in the name of that company. Many agents and solicitors are around to see you through this process. The process of buying will, it is hoped, become easier as Bulgaria is harmonised into the EU.

If you intend to buy a property off-plan or new build then you have to check that the developer has all the necessary permissions in place. They should also be an experienced developer. As in England, there are cowboys about! Several developers are offering rental guarantee schemes. However, make sure that you check this carefully. Given the rapid rate of development it is vital to check to see if the rental market is there or whether you are simply paying for the rental guarantee in the purchase price.

Estate agents

Estate agents are not regulated in Bulgaria so always check carefully before you enter into a deal. The best case scenario is to find a UK based agent specialising in Bulgarian property.

Costs of buying in Bulgaria

At the time of writing, the following are the costs associated with buying a property in Bulgaria:

- Agents costs-the buyer pays commission which can be between 3-5% of purchase price
- Company registration fee-as mentioned, foreigners cannot buy land so many form a company to buy both buildings and land. You will need to pay a deposit of 1800 euros and a minimum of 2500 euros into the company bank account. Once the company is formed you will have access to this money but the cost of forming the company will be around 750 euros
- Lawyers fees-this amounts to 1%, depending on what the lawyer is required to do
- State or local tax-this is equivalent of UK stamp duty and is approximately 2-4% of the property price. It may vary according to the location of the property as it is set by the local municipality
- Land registry or property tax-this covers the cost of registering the title deeds with the municipality and is 0.15% of the purchase price
- Notary fees-these will amount to around 200-300 euros for witnessing the purchase deeds
- Translators fees-you may require your documents to be translated into English-these will be around £50

- Surveyors fees-these are optional and will vary with the type of property

There is no VAT on the purchase of property in Bulgaria.

You should regard Bulgaria as a long-term investment as prices will not rise quickly again for a good few years as supply now easily exceeds demand. Don't listen to the wild claims of people who are interested only in getting properties off their hands. Remember, nowhere is immune from the credit crunch. Make sure that you do your homework before buying anything. There are many websites dedicated to buying property in Bulgaria and many that give case histories. Some are listed at the end of this chapter.

Romania

The accession of Romania into the European Community in 2007 has meant that there are many rapid changes in the country which will attract property investors. As Bulgaria has become the new Spain (lets hope not) so Romania is set to become the new Bulgaria, so the saying goes. There are plans for new airports and roads and there is expected to be a relocation of industry to Romania where favourable conditions exist. This in turn will bring prosperity and land and property will rise in value.

There are no restrictions on foreign nationals acquiring dwellings in Romania. Ownership of land is tricky, but companies incorporated in Romania as well as resident foreign nationals and non-resident EU citizens can acquire land.

The actual purchase of property in Romania is bedevilled by red tape and it is for this reason that it is essential to buy through an established Romanian property company and to employ an English speaking Romanian lawyer. It is also, as elsewhere in ex-communist countries, imperative to establish title, as land and properties were seized during the Ceausescu era. There is always a chance, especially when buying older properties, that the property may be claimed by its original owner.

The choice of properties in Romania consists mainly of resale homes and new build although planning restrictions are currently tight limiting the amount of new build on the market. The current costs of property in Romania in 2019 are:

- In **Bucharest** the average selling price of apartments rose by 6.04% (2.93% inflation-adjusted) y-o-y to €1,335 (US$ 1,525) per sq. m.

- In **Cluj-Napoca**, Romania's fourth most populous city, apartment prices sharply rose by 6.73% (3.6% inflation-adjusted) y-o-y to €1,555 (US$ 1,776) per sq. m.

- In **Timisoara**, the average selling price of apartments went up by 4.77% (1.7% inflation-adjusted) to €1,207 (US$ 1,378) per sq. m.

- In **Brasov**, the average selling price of apartments soared 9.43% (6.23% inflation-adjusted) to €1,102 (US$ 1,258) per sq. m.

- In **Constanta**, the country's oldest city, apartment prices rose by just 2.01% (fell by 0.98% when adjusted for inflation) to €1,117 (US$ 1,276) per sq. m.

The capital of Romania, Bucharest, is only two hours away by air from the UK. The cost of living is low. The country as a whole looks attractive for future investment with new build apartments starting from £30,000 rising depending on size and location. There are estate agents springing up which will steer people through the Romanian legal system.

Rental yields

Moderate to good rental yields in Bucharest, Romania

How much can you earn? Bucharest's rental yields are good: a **120 sq.m. apartment** can rent for about 950 euros per month, earning a rental yield of 6.1%.

- a **70 sq. m. apartment** can rent for about 550 euros per month, earning a rental yield of 6.1%

The Baltic States

The countries of the Baltic States, Lithuania, Estonia and Latvia are architectural gems and have only relatively recently been invaded by tourists and property speculators, including second-homers.

Until recently the Baltic States of Latvia, Lithuania and Estonia were hardly visited by British tourists. Joining the EU in

May 2004 opened a lot of doors for the Baltics, and property investors took advantage of these three burgeoning economies.

The story of the Baltic States is really one of size, and it has been thanks to such manageable land mass that all three countries achieved such an awful lot in a short space of time. Hopes that Estonia will be the first nation on earth to become completely wireless gives you an idea of where these countries are headed.

NATO membership and currencies that are pegged to the euro completed the package, while low interest rates and falling inflation encouraged the locals to get onto the property ladder. Despite being slow starters in the property game (nationals were only permitted to buy their own homes in the early 1990s), prices in the Baltics fast approached Western levels. However, in the past couple of years a combination of a drop in interest from European buyers as credit conditions tighten and an oversupply of new property has forced prices down.

Popular buying locations

The capital cities of Tallinn, Vilnius and Riga are where most British buyers have been looking, lured by strong capital appreciation and regular rental income. These three cities are hot on Prague's heels in terms of a budget weekend destination, a fact which compliments the established long-term rental market extremely well. Rents in the capitals are falling and need to be closely examined if you are looking for the property to support itself, but still remain relatively good

Having said that, coastal resorts near the city centres have also proved popular with investors. Located just an hour's drive south of Tallinn is Parnu – Estonia's 'summer capital'. Property prices here are around 30 per cent cheaper that in Tallinn itself, and the resort offers two golf courses and several spas to boot.

In Latvia, the town of Saliena, just five kilometres from Riga, is well placed for commuters. It is the recipient of some well designed master-planning, and the old port is now a bustling residential centre. Meanwhile, Lithuania's second city of Kaunas offers a good alternative to the capital, offering bustling nightlife at more reasonable prices.

Legal issues

There are no restrictions on the type of property that you are able to purchase, however some buildings may be protected under heritage regulations. If you buy a resale property in an old town, there could be rules which you will need to abide by regarding renovation.

There have been instances of some resale homes being sold without the correct title deeds, but this isn't a problem that can't be avoided with the use of an independent solicitor. Be aware that the purchase contract is highly likely to be in the local language, so if your solicitor is not bilingual you will need to arrange for a professional translation.

If you are buying a new-build home, the final contact will not be signed until the property has been completed – usually around 12 to 18 months later – but this probably won't deter many developers from charging stage payments throughout the build. If this is the case, make sure that all financial transactions are legally documented.

If buying in a city centre, you will more likely than not be purchasing an apartment. In this instance, it is a good idea to get your lawyer to check over the management contract before you sign anything. Maintenance fees are usually divided by the whole block, so it is important to ensure that, if you are buying a studio, you are not paying the same monthly service fees as the three-bedroom penthouse.

The buying process

The Baltic States rely on a notary system, similar to that in France. Despite this representation, it is essential that you employ independent legal advice from a solicitor who acts solely on your behalf.

When you have found a property that you wish to buy, you will need to put in an offer through an estate agent – much as you would in the UK. When the offer is accepted you will be required to pay a reservation fee of around €1,000 (around £900), shortly followed by a deposit of around ten per cent. As soon as you have paid the reservation fee you are legally bound to the purchase – there is no cooling off period.

Both parties sign the final contract in the presence of the notary, who then registers the new title deeds with the relevant authorities. Transfer of title can take as little as four weeks, but the time scale really depends on how quickly you are able to make an appointment with the notary.

Finance

Local mortgages are available at competitive rates, usually from around 3.5 per cent, and finance is available for up to 100 per cent of the purchase price – although 85 to 90 per cent is more common. The mortgage market is a highly competitive one as more locals realise the benefits of such financing options, though global credit restrictions have caused the stream of credit to slow considerably.

The loan issued will depend on your ability to repay the mortgage, as well as the type of property that you are hoping to secure it against, and it will be conditional on the property being correctly insured. You may find it easier to get a mortgage on a new home but all properties, even if they are new-build, will have to pass a bank valuation. However, be aware that terms and conditions change depending on how many properties you own – local banks are unlikely to lend more than 50 per cent LTV (loan to value) for any successive properties.

Fees and taxes

You will need to budget for notary fees of around €250, land registration fees of €100, valuation fees of €100, mortgage arrangement fees of one per cent, and relevant insurance costs. A two per cent purchase tax will also need to be paid before the property is registered at the land registry.

In Estonia you will have to pay 26 per cent tax on a second home that is bought as an investment property. You will also be liable for Land Tax, which is paid on the market value of any land that you own on a yearly basis.

Estate agents fees vary between three and seven per cent, and you may have to pay these when buying as well as when selling. In Latvia there is no capital gains tax, provided that you have owned the property for at least a year, and the CGT thresholds are currently being reduced in Estonia and Lithuania. There is no inheritance tax in any of the Baltic States, but there is no guarantee that this won't change.

Visas, residency and work permits

British citizens do not require a visa to visit the Baltic States as they are all members of the European Union, however you may need to declare yourself resident for tax purposes if you live there full time. Residency is determined by the number of days spent in the country. People who spend more that 183 days in a calendar year, or who have a permanent home in the country, are considered to be tax residents. The UK currently has a double tax treaty with Estonia.

Again, keep an eye on the situation Post Brexit as it will change.

If you are planning on living and working in Estonia on a permanent basis you may need to obtain a Business Visa before you enter the country. Once you have been granted a Business Visa you will need to prove that you have health insurance to the value of £15,000 before you are granted entry.

New-build versus resale

Be aware that new-build property in the Baltic States is not delivered as it is in the UK – it is normally sold in what is called a 'grey finished state'. This means that you simply inherit an empty shell, with bare concrete floors and walls that haven't even been plastered. Occasionally you may purchase a property that's in a 'white finished state', and while this will have plastered walls, flooring and doors, you will still need to install both a bathroom and a kitchen as well as decorate the property.

Although labour is much cheaper in the Baltic's, as a rule of thumb you will need to budget around €10,000 to get your property into a habitable state.

Resale homes are likely to be more expensive than their new-build counterparts. This is because they tend to be situated nearer the old city centres which command the premium prices. They also don't come with the two-year guarantee of new-builds.

Investment potential

The Knight Frank Global House Index for the first quarter of 2006 cited that house prices in Estonia rose by an impressive 17 per cent – making it the fastest growing property market in the world at the time. Since then, prices rises have slowed and even started to come down as international buyers become scarcer, global credit flows slow down and the oversupply of property in the cities takes hold. In Tallinn however, investors can still expect to see rental returns to range between four and seven per cent.

Latvia has perhaps suffered some of the worst drops in property prices of all of the emerging markets since their peak level in April 2007 – some figures put the drop since then at up to 45 per cent in Riga. The trouble of the finance and banking sectors has caused a degree of chaos in the housing market, and as the economic struggles have now spilled into the political arena, further instability could be on the cards in the future. However, some will see the drop in prices as a blessing for the future of real estate in Latvia, bring prices down to more realistic levels and offering a little more value to buyers when they are attracted back into the market.

There was a similar story in Lithuania, as prices peaked in early 2007 and then began to fall back. Average price drops have been around 29 per cent when the higher rate of inflation in Lithuania is taken into account. GDP growth is still continuing in the Baltics, although at a much slower rate than was previously the case, but it is difficult to make a case for short-term investment in the property market at the present time.

Health and education

No vaccinations are required before travelling to the Baltic States, but ensure that you take out comprehensive medical insurance as, while the private health sectors have a good reputation, the public hospitals aren't so well organised.

Education is largely hindered by the language barrier. While English is widely spoken in the Baltic States, it is not the primary language in schools and, so, while education is of a high standard, it is probably best to continue to educate your child in Britain unless they are young enough to easily absorb a complex second language.

Transport

easyJet flies into Tallinn, as does the national carrier Estonian Air. Once in the city, there is a range of hire care firms available if you wish to drive, which is on the right. If you preferred that somebody else did the navigating, there are always taxis available, while buses, trolleybuses and trams provide an even cheaper alternative.

Riga is perhaps the most accessible of the three capitals, as it is serviced by easyJet, Ryanair, BA and Lufthansa. Latvia has a good road network, and is home to the Via Baltica – one of the largest infrastructure projects currently underway in the Baltic's. A national rail service connects the major cities of Latvia for a reasonable price, although it is perhaps not the country's quickest mode of transport.

In Lithuania, Air Baltic flies into Vilnius, while Ryanair services Kaunas. Once on the ground, Lithuania's major roads have a good reputation, with Vilnius, Kaunas and Klaipeda being linked by a modern motorway. If driving, be aware that the Lithuanian's have zero-tolerance for drinking and driving.

And finally...

It is unlikely that the Baltic States will become any more than a weekend-break destination due to their climate. Mild, fresh summers are succeeded by bitterly cold winters that rarely break freezing point. It is also extremely dark from October to March, meaning that Estonia, Latvia and Lithuania are unlikely to attract many full-time expats.

The language barrier can also be a tough one to break, with many Brits struggling to make head nor tale of the local dialects. And, while the capitals of Tallinn, Riga and Vilnius offer a cosmopolitan dining scene, you may struggle to get more than the traditional fare of pork and potatoes the further afield you travel.

It is also possible that the city centres are at risk of over development and oversupply has been a problems in all three capital cities. While the local market was strong, prices continued to rise at a hectic pace. Since then, the locals have been priced out of the market – therefore affecting resale potential.

The Czech Republic

Prague has been established for many years now as an investor hot spot with other areas outside the capital lagging behind. Membership of the European Union has already had a major effect on foreign property ownership. As with Bulgaria and Romania, it was necessary to form a company to own land. However, in the Czech Republic after 2004, it became possible to own land subject to being granted a residency permit. You will need a lawyer to obtain this for you. Taxes are low but there is a 3% transfer tax when you buy a property. Prices are not appreciating as rapidly as the Baltic States because the Czech Republic has flattened out somewhat, much the same as Bulgaria.

Slovenia

Slovenia is a tiny country with less than 2 million inhabitants but is rapidly becoming a popular tourist destination. It has good beaches, good climate and also has skiing in winter. One day it may have golf! Very few foreigners have yet bought property in Slovenia but this will change, so it is a country to keep an eye on.

Poland

It is in the capital, Warsaw, where property values have risen the most, with Krakow following close second. Like Lithuania, properties are often sold without interiors and it is up to the homeowner to finish the job in order to make the property inhabitable. People have been investing in Poland for a while now and mortgages are readily available for foreigners, although it is unlikely that a UK bank would provide a mortgage, and specialist credit brokers would need to be approached. Only Poles can currently purchase land in Poland for building or otherwise. It is possible to buy land **if** you have a company or if a holding company buys on your behalf. Land prices have been rising steadily in Poland over the last few years but it can still be very cheap compared to other parts of Europe.

Costs of buying a property in Poland are quite low with agents fee of around 3%, stamp duty of 2%, lawyers fees of about 1% and between £3,500-£6000 to register a property depending on value.

Once the property has been owned by the same person for five years, there is no capital gains tax to be paid by foreign investors. 19% has to be paid if a sale is within five years. However, advice should be taken on this as there is a degree of ambiguity.

As with all ex-communist countries it is absolutely essential to establish title to a communist era property.

Many older properties in Poland are in need of renovation. Buyers are advised to choose a property that is being renovated by established builders or to buy new build.

Like everything, you need experience of Poland and its culture before embarking on any complex project. There are companies who can help, listed at the end of this chapter.

Poland has a double taxation treaty with the UK, which means that you will not be taxed twice on any tax you pay in Poland. It is very advisable to open a Polish bank account when purchasing property in Poland.

Slovakia

This country, although beautiful, has a weak economy and is considered high risk for investors. Since Slovakia's accession to the EU, the government has been actively encouraging foreign property investment through devices such as waiving stamp duty. This, together with low prices, makes investment attractive. Two bed apartments can be bought for £50,000 and developers offer a guaranteed rental income of around 7%. As with all such guarantees you need to be sure that there is a demand. The capital Bratislava is beautiful and close to Vienna, sitting next to the Danube. If sense can be made of the system of purchasing property, and estate agencies are beginning to appear, then it is considered to be a worthwhile investment for the future.

How to Buy

Appointing an independent lawyer rather than someone chosen by the estate agent is strongly recommended, as is a structural survey, unless it's a new build. Deposits between 10 and 20% are usual and will secure a property, after which completion is usually relatively quick – about three to four weeks. If you pull out after signing the pre-purchase agreement that goes with the deposit, the seller can deduct expenses before returning the balance of the deposit. If they pull out, you get it back in full. As with many other emerging markets, the key items for the lawyer to check are that the seller truly owns the property outright and that there are no debts secured on it.

As there's no stamp duty or property transfer tax in Slovakia, the only extras are the fees for the lawyer (around €500) and land registration fees (about the same). Vat is 19% and is levied on land and buildings that are less than five years old. And although there's no capital gains tax (CGT) as such, the gain is taxed as income at the flat rate of 20%. This rate is also levied on any rental income and there is a tax treaty with the United Kingdom so if you decide to pay in Slovakia, you won't be taxed back home as well.

There's a broad range of property available in Slovakia and the chances are that, whatever type of investment you are making, if you choose the location and property carefully you have every right to expect a significant rise in value over the next few years. Have a look around, do your research and you won't go wrong.

Hungary

Hungary is an increasingly popular country to buy, especially in Budapest, with District V being the most popular area. The city is beautiful, quite staggeringly so, sitting on the Danube. Hungary has always been the most progressive of countries, especially since the latter days of communist rule, and there is a healthy dislike, particularly among the older generation, of their ex communist master, Russia. The country has a well-developed legal system and there are many estate agents based there.

The majority of property sales are apartments and many of these are very spacious and well finished. It is not so easy to obtain mortgages there, especially now, and many cash buyers have been involved in purchase and rental. Foreign buyers have to apply to the local authority to purchase a home and it is essential that good sound legal advice is obtained before entering into an investment.

Croatia

An alternative to the more classic Mediterranean destinations but with a twist of Italian, Croatia offers a breathtaking coastline dotted with family-friendly resorts. With one of the prettiest coastlines in the Med – thanks to its thousands of unspoilt islands and waterside Venetian architecture – Croatia has always been popular with sailing enthusiasts.

Since 2009, the country has welcomed foreign house-hunters to its shores after it changed its restrictive ownership laws to allow people from all EU countries to own property there (without the hassle of having to do so through a company, which is what Brits had to do). Keep an eye on BREXIT!

Property hotspots in Croatia

Istria wasn't dubbed the "New Tuscany" for nothing, and it was its proximity to the Italian border combined with its distinctive – and familiar – Italian feel, that first attracted British buyers to buy in Croatia at all.

Novigrad, a charming resort half an hour drive from the border, is a good starting point in northern Istria and has properties ranging from traditional homes overlooking the Adriatic to large villas on the edge of town, priced from around €350,000. Heading south along the Istrian coast takes you to Porec and then Rovinj, both with similar appeal and buying opportunities to Novigrad. If you want to be closer to the airport in southern Istria at Pula – served by Ryanair – the seaside town of Premantura has much to offer.

Another interesting area is the South Dalmatian coast, specifically a stretch that takes in the resorts of Vodice, Primosten, built on a peninsula and regarded as Dalmatia's most picturesque resort, and Rogoznica, 30 kilometres from Split's airport (which is actually at Trogir). Vodice is typical of all three – a family resort set around a historic centre of old stone buildings, with a marina, small harbour and long promenade. High-rise blocks are not allowed, so property available includes villas and small apartment complexes.

Split and the nearby islands have also become popular in recent years, with the islands of Hvar and Brac especially fashionable. Apartments in grand renovated buildings around the beautiful old palace of Split are more affordable than comparables in Dubrovnik's old town.

Dubovnik needs little introduction, already a popular long weekend destination. Buying a home around the city centre, while it would make an exciting city pad and have huge rental appeal – is expensive.

The process of buying a property in Croatia

You may need to be patient, as getting the necessary permissions to buy a property in Croatia can take a year, or more. That is why many buyers have gone down the route of buying via a company, which is quicker but can be more expensive in corporate taxes and hassle. Moreover, with title sometimes hard to establish after the chaos and dispora following the break-up of Yugoslavia, it is often better to take things slower. You will be required to give a 10 per cent deposit along with the preliminary contract. In the boom years vendors often asked for the entire payment to be paid on deposit, which may sound outrageous but can make sense, because (a) the vendor will often allow you to move into the property in the meantime and (b) because the vendor must pay you twice the deposit amount if they decide to pull out - for example after getting a better offer.

When the Ministry of Foreign Affairs approves you, the final contracts are signed before the notary (all agreements you sign must be translated and notarised) and taxes/fees paid.

Buying costs

Buying costs in Croatia include agent's fees, typically between two and four per cent, stamp duty of five per cent and notary costs of around €50 and another €40 for registering ownership. Legal fees depend on the value of the property and can vary from €1,000-€3,000.

Buyer beware:

The Croatian bureaucracy has a bad reputation, not only for inefficiency but also for stroppily putting your application to the back of the queue if you make even a small mistake. It is therefore wise to have a highly switched on local solicitor to speed your application to the Ministry of Foreign Affairs and ensure that every i is dotted and t crossed.

*

Useful Information

Bulgaria

Properties in Bulgaria

www.propertiesinbulgaria.com

BulgarianProperties.com/Bulgaria

www.gov.uk/guidance/how-to-buy-property-in-bulgaria

investmentproperty.co.uk › overseasproperty

Lithuania

www.globalpropertyguide.com/Europe/Lithuania/Buying-Guide

www.rightmove.co.uk/overseas-property/in-Lithuania.html

Estonia and Latvia

www.globalpropertyguide.com/Europe/Latvia/Buying-Guide

Ober-Haus Estate Agents

www.ober-haus.com

tallinn-property.goodsonandred.com/2012/07/ten-top-tips-when-buying-residential...

Czech Republic

www.property-abroad.com/czech-republic/buyers-guide

*www.global*prope**rty***guide.com/Europe/*Czech-Republic/*Buying-
Guide

Poland

www.buyinghousepoland.co.uk

www.property-abroad.com/poland/buyers-guide

Romania

www.wikihow.com/Buy-a-Property-in-romania

www.globalpropertyguide.com/Europe/Romania/Buying-Guide

Hungary

https://www.property-abroad.com/hungary

www.properties-in-hungary.co.uk/buying-property-in-
hungary.php

Slovakia

www.rightmove.co.uk/*overseas-property/*in-Slovakia.*html*

/*www.globalpropertyguide.com/Europe/***Slovak**-
*Republic/*Buying-*Guide*

Culture Ministry Website

www.pamiatky.sk

Slovenia

www.slovenianproperties.com

www.thinkslovenia.com/slovenia-property.php

www.globalpropertyguide.com/Europe/Slovenia/Buying-Guide

Croatia

www.croatiapropertysales.com/buy

www.property-abroad.com/croatia/buyers-guide

www.globalpropertyguide.com/Europe/Croatia/Buying-Guide

www.croatiapropertysales.com/about

****

Chapter 13

Other Second Home and Investment Opportunities

There are numerous other countries in the world where property investment and second homing is proving popular. Obviously in a book this size I cannot cover the entire planet. However, a good proportion of the known world is covered. In this chapter, I will look at Turkey, Morocco, Brazil, South Africa, New Zealand, Australia and Thailand.

Turkey

Over the last ten years or so, Turkey has become more and more popular with package tours, and also individual travellers. It has certainly become more popular since I was last there during the good old days of the Magic Bus and the hippy trail to India (which I completed I am proud to say). Back in the 1970's it wasn't as developed as it is now but I am pleased to say that the process of over-development that has blighted European countries hasn't really occurred there.

The process of investing in property in Turkey remains precarious because of the lack of a reliable local legal system for dealing with property transactions. Estate agents are beginning to establish themselves but are still in their infancy. Stories abound of people buying property and finding that they have purchased something with no proper title. However, so saying this, the country is attracting investors because of its beautiful coastline and its historical attractions.

The main area for investment in Turkey is the Bodrum peninsula which is becoming more expensive as time goes on. It has a very good climate and is quite sophisticated and the property is still relatively cheap, with apartments available from around £75,000.

At the moment, Turkey is still trying to gain membership of the EU, which is still uncertain. If it does manage this then property will increase rapidly in value as there is good access from Europe in general.

There are around 10,000 British people resident in Turkey and around 70,000 have second homes there. Price rises have been rapid in recent years. However, as mentioned, the legal system is fragile and the amount of red tape when purchasing and establishing title to a property is enormous.

If you are considering Turkey as a destination and potential investment, you should make sure that you use an agency that is a member of FOPDAC (Federation of Overseas Property developers Agents and Consultants). This is important when dealing with property purchase in any country as FOPDAC's members have to abide by a code of practice. You should make sure that you never deal directly with sellers and that you intend to hold the property for a minimum of four years, after which there is no capital gains tax payable. Mortgages for property purchase in Turkey, from local banks, are not available so you would need to arrange this in the UK.

The best places to invest in Turkey lie in areas that are being developed, i.e. new roads and airports are being built along with sports facilities.

Buying process

Once you have found a suitable property you need to find an independent lawyer. Your lawyer should be shown all the relevant legal paperwork, the TAPU (title deeds) and Iskan (habitation licence) before you proceed any further. He will check the property can be sold to a non-Turkish buyer and discuss the basics of how and when you are going to pay for your property. Usually a holding deposit will be required, which varies according to the area and the seller, but is typically £2,000 to £3,000. A date for a full 10 to 30 per cent deposit will be agreed (less the holding deposit). You will need to get a tax number and open a bank account.

Typically, the buying process can take just eight weeks. Many sellers will accept the balance of the asking price (70 to 90 per cent) once the process has been completed and deeds including Iskan are ready for issue. These terms will vary depending on whether you are buying a re-sale, new build or off-plan property. Taxes, connection fees and buyer's tax will also be payable at the deed issue time. The solicitor can then put all the payment items into a contract, with all the relevant legal sections to it including

145

the interested parties' details, payment plan details and legal references to the delivery of the property.

Once complete, the parties sign all the pages of a Turkish contract, which is translated into English by a licensed translator. Once this is done and the deposit received, your application papers will be sent for military clearance, before the deeds can then be issued into the buyer's name. At this stage if you decide you are not returning to Turkey to sign for your deeds, you can get to a UK-based notary to appoint the lawyer to sign on your behalf for your deeds.

Buying costs

Buying costs will vary between regions of Turkey, but as a guide, allow for at least £1000 for your Turkey-based legal fees. The Notary costs (including Power of Attorney) are from £200.

Property Purchase Tax (like stamp duty) will be 3.3 per cent of the total of the registered purchase price. The Land Registry cost is £125. Estate agency fees for re-sale property are generally 3 per cent, and utility transfer fees from £150.

Buyer beware:

Buyers have been known to slip up, especially if they don't have a truly independent lawyer who can do all the proper checks. Do not use one that is beholden to the developer.

For off-plan purchases, if the property is currently being built, only agree to make payments against actual delivery of the build, not an arbitrary date passing. Check who will be responsible for maintenance once you have purchased the property.

Morocco

Morocco is very quickly becoming a property hotspot. There is now a budget airline, Ryanair, and others are following. The country has a tradition of writers and artists settling there and has a reputation of bohemianism. However, more and more investors are circling around with the aim of opening the country up and, of course, make a profit. New developments are going up outside of popular and well-known places like Marrakech, along the lesser known coastlines. There is a strong rental demand all year round. You would need the services of local agents who are well versed with the country's systems.

Buying process

Morocco uses a French system of property buying, so you will need to find a notaire as well as an independent solicitor.

When your initial verbal offer has been accepted you sign a legally binding preliminary offer and pay a 10 per cent deposit for a resale home, up to 40 per cent for off-plan.

Although new builds are fairly straightforward, as in some other north African countries, getting clear title can be an issue for older properties where many family members must be traced and must agree to the sale, taking as long as a year. A month before completion, you will be sent the final contract to sign before the notaire (or allow your lawyer to sign with power of attorney) and when the final contract is signed you also pay over the remaining purchase price, fees and taxes.

Buying costs

Purchase costs are around six per cent. Not widely available yet, mortgages are around 70% per cent LTV, with a maximum 20 year term and rate of five to 10 per cent.

Buyer beware:

Buying new-build is at least ten times more straightforward than buying an ancient home with melkia (pre-Land Registry) title – these commonly have multiple owners (maybe 100) with all having to agree to a sale; often a protracted nightmare for the unwary!

Brazil

Foreign investment is Brazil is increasing. Once the domain of the wealthy, or the adventurous, the country is opening up to anyone who can afford to get there. Prices are still relatively low. One popular place is Bahia, where the government is investing heavily and where you can buy an apartment from £40,000. However, prices are rising fast. In order to buy in Brazil, you have to obtain a personal identification number. Having done this you then set up a bank account in the country. Most developers of repute will be able to steer you through the buying process. The legal systems are quite well established and there are no real problems with title.

Buying process

Getting a mortgage in Brazil is difficult, and as a foreigner your options might be limited. Taking local advice from a specialist is essential . so if you need to borrow to fund your purchase you are better off funding your property from home.

Always double check anything an estate agent or developer tells you (there was a fair amount of artistic license in descriptions of lavish new developments during the boom, many of which have never since been built), do your own due diligence and ask for corroborating documents. Check the developer's track record and building licence.

Buying costs

Buying costs include transfer taxes of around three to five per cent (though this varies from state to state, and is generally higher by the seafront) and fees to the notary of around two per cent. For legal fees (which are essential to guarantee clear title) you should budget for around £1000. Estate agent fees are paid by the seller.

Buyer beware:

Foreigners without permanent residency cannot open bank accounts in Brazil and sending money can be complex. If you send money to a developer, all transfers into Brazil pass through the Banco Central, which belongs to the Government. They will only forward the payment to the recipient if there is paperwork to justify the transfer, so you always need a signed contract to transfer money.

You can't buy Brazilian currency outside the country, so you need to send funds in your home currency and it is converted at the Central Bank rate when it reaches Brazil. Use a specialist foreign exchange company such as Moneycorp, who partners with a Brazilian exchange bank..

South Africa

South Africa, released from the shackles of apartheid, is rapidly becoming a popular second home location for well- heeled investors. Most properties offered in South Africa are well built and are within gated complexes. There are currently low interest rates, low inflation and good climate. There are beautiful mountain ranges and national parks such as the Kruger National Park. However, there is still the sense of political instability. It takes a long time to shake off the evils of the apartheid system. Shantytowns with high levels of poverty and deprivation exist.

Property prices are relatively expensive, as might be expected with the levels of security needed. However, by comparison with the UK you get more for your money, with a five bed house in cape Town with sea views, pool and garage costing around £500,000. There are many properties under this price tag, with location and amenities underpinning prices, as everywhere.

The east coast of South Africa is semi-tropical, much like Florida and is also humid in the Summer. Overall, the climate is good year round.

EU citizens can stay in South Africa for up to six months at a time as long as they can prove support and have a return ticket. Anyone who wishes to stay for a longer time needs a residency permit, and an employment permit if they intend to work there. If property has already been bought in South Africa this will count towards your residency permit. Income tax is payable only on income earned in the country and there is a top rate of 45%. Health care is good, although private health insurance is advised.

There are many types of property available in South Africa, from coastal properties, mansions and game lodges. All money that is brought into the country must go through the South African reserve bank although all money made from sale of property can be taken out of the country.

The process of buying a property in South Africa

The buying process is very similar to the UK but with small differences. Once you have exchanged contracts you cannot pull out without losing your deposit. There are no restrictions on foreign ownership (assuming you have no criminal record) but it is best to use a legal conveyancer who specialises in foreign property transactions.

Transfer and mortgage documents can be signed overseas at a South African embassy or at the offices of a notary public. VAT is only applicable if the seller is a VAT vendor, otherwise transfer duty is applicable. Bear in mind that sellers need to pay agent's fees which are generally subject to VAT.

Buying costs
Fees and Taxes

The following fees and taxes must be paid by the seller: real estate brokerage fees: normally 5 percent of the market value of the property (dictated by the agreement between the parties). Urban and rural real estate brokerage fees: between 5 percent and 10 percent of the total property value. Real estate fees for properties in construction: between 5 percent and 8 percent

The purchaser

Before signing a preliminary contract, check exactly what fees are payable and have them confirmed in writing.

In addition to the fees associated with buying a home, you must also take into account the running costs. These include local property taxes, building insurance, contents insurance, standing charges for utilities, community fees for a community property, garden and pool maintenance costs, and a caretaker's or management fees if you leave a home empty or let it. Annual running costs usually average around 2 to 4 per cent of the cost of a property.

Transfer Duty

Transfer duty is a tax levied on the transfer of ownership of fixed property. If you are buying as a company, a close corporation or a trust (sometimes called a 'legal entity'), transfer duty is levied at a flat rate of 10 per cent of the purchase price. If you are buying as an individual (officially termed a 'natural person'), duty is calculated on the following scale: If you buy a home in South Africa, you must pay transfer duty on the value of the property above R500,000 (€51,840). Duty is levied at 5 per cent on the value between R5000,000 and R1,000,000 (€103,680), and at 8 per cent on any value over R1,000,000.

Value (R)	Duty Rate (%)	Cumulative Duty (R)
Up to 500,000	0	
500,001 – 1,000,000	5	
Over 1,000,000	8	25,000

If you are buying a property to a developer registered in VAT (Value Added Tax), you will pay VAT instead of the transfer duty.

Legal Or Conveyancing Fees

These are calculated on a sliding scale and amount to between 1 and 2 per cent of the purchase price, depending on the value of the property.

Bank & Mortgage Costs

Bank inspection fees are around 0.2 per cent of the valuation, and the mortgage arrangement fee is around 1 to 1.5 per cent of the loan amount.

Utility Fees

If you buy a new property, you must usually pay for electricity and water connections (and occasionally gas, but it's little used in South Africa) and the installation of meters. You should ask the builder or developer to provide the cost of connection to services in writing. If you buy a resale property, you must usually pay for the cost of new contracts, particularly water.

Other Fees

Other fees may include surveyor's or inspection fees, architect's fees and the cost of moving house.

Note that stamp duty was abolished in the 2004 budget but is still (erroneously) mentioned on many websites dealing with buying property in South Africa

Buyer beware

Non-residents of SA who do not have, or wish to acquire, permanent residence may buy property outright for cash and will be granted a 90-day visa, with possible extensions for each visit. Intending immigrants who have already applied for permanent residence and who have funds in transit to SA may qualify for a mortgage of up to 50 per cent of the value of any property they wish to buy.

Bear in mind that it can be tricky getting your money out of South Africa when you want to sell up; also that crime remains a big problem in cities such as Cape Town, whatever people say.

Most homes have hefty security gates/grilles and have rapid-response alarm systems linked to the police.

Australia

The process of foreign investors buying a property anywhere in Australia is rather more complicated than most people think. Any foreign investor, regardless of scale of investment, has to seek approval through what is known as the Foreign Investment Review Board. If you hold a permanent visa then you can purchase residential property.

However, if the intended purchase is a holiday home then the restrictions may not apply if you are intending to buy in what is known as an 'integrated tourism resort'. Timeshare property is regarded as an investment in residential property and a visitor is generally not allowed to spend more than four weeks a year in the property. If you remain for more than six months a year in Australia you will become liable for Australian income tax.

Mortgages are not available for Australian properties from UK banks. Australian banks will lend subject to the usual restrictions.

Process of buying a property in Australia

Australians have traditionally been more likely to buy a property at auction, with as many as 65 to 80 per cent buying in this way.

An alternative to finding a property yourself is to employ a buyers' agents who not only find your property for you, but also help to negotiate for it, in return for one to two per cent of the purchase price.

In some states buyers simply employ a conveyancing clerk rather than a lawyer; the process usually taking one to three months from start to finish.

First home owner grant

The first homeowner grant (FHOG) is designed to help young people get on the property ladder. The grant is usually set at AUD$7,000 (£4,380), though it can vary. Still, it is a good chunk of the bill for a first-time buyer and is open to Brits, too, as long as they have never owned property in Australia before.

Buying costs

Buying costs are about four per cent on houses and land and six per cent on apartments, but vary from state to state, as do the processes. The biggest cost is usually stamp duty, of 1.25 to 6.75 per cent. Legal costs add up to two per cent; due diligence such as building inspection costs AUD$300- AUD$500 [£185-£310] and 'strata' inspections (on apartments) adds AUD$200-AUD$500 [£125-£310]. It adds to anywhere between two and nine per cent, not dissimilar to selling costs, where the highest cost is estate agent fees.

Buyer beware

To secure your life in Australia you need to get a visa. It's worth applying for one through an emigration agent, one that is a registered with the Migration Agents Registration Authority (MARA) and/or is a member of the Migration Institute of Australia (MIA). There are three common visa routes. First, there is the Skilled Independent visa: this is for under 50-year-olds who have skills that meet the Australian standard for an occupation on the Skills Occupation List – this currently includes accountants, healthcare professionals and bricklayers. Second is the Skilled Sponsored visa: this is similar to the Skilled Independent visa, but to qualify you must be sponsored by a relative in Australia or be nominated by a state or government agency. Third is the Skilled Regional Sponsored visa: this is a three-year visa for skilled workers who are unable to get a Skilled Independent visa although you can apply for permanent residency after two years and after working at least 12 months in a 'specified regional area'. Visa eligibility is based on a points system. There are also fairly steep charges for Australian visas, in excess of AUD$7,000 and the application process can take 3 years. To find out more about visas and if your occupation is in demand in Australia visit www.immi.gov.au

New Zealand

New Zealand is a vast country with wide open spaces, good climate, lower healthcare costs and more and more Britons are buying property there. Britons can purchase most kinds of property. However, to buy a property in a desirable location such as an island or a beachfront property permission has to be granted by New Zealand's Overseas Investment Commission.

There is no stamp duty or capital gains tax, unless the property is traded as a business. The average time to complete a sale is four weeks. City centres provide new build homes but outside of the city you would work with a developer to design and build your own home.

New Zealand is vibrant at the moment, particularly places like Auckland which have a thriving rental market. As with cities all over the world the waterfront is being developed and property prices are on the rise. Wellington is similar, with huge growth in property prices in recent years.

The process of buying a property in New Zealand

Buying a property in NZ is a lot like buying a house in the UK. You find a home you like, put in an offer – once the mortgage is arranged and searches and surveys carried out, you'll pay a ten per cent deposit and sign a contract. However, completion usually takes place three weeks after signing the contract – which is legally binding – and it's unusual for there to be delays.

You can apply for a mortgage before or after you emigrate to New Zealand. Banks will look at three things: your income, your deposit and your commitments. Having the paperwork that demonstrates those three things makes the process easier. Bringing your old employment contract from the UK to show that you have a similar income in a comparable industry will help, as will statements from previous home loans to show borrowing history.

Buying costs

There is no stamp duty, inheritance tax of capital gains tax in New Zealand but you will have to budget around £475 for solicitors fees, £140 for a valuation fee, £150 for a building inspection report, £50 for the Land Information Memorandum and a transfer fee of around £20.

Buyer beware

The New Zealand government's rigorous immigration process is considered by many to be even harder than Australia's, not least because their application rules change on a weekly basis and they don't allow British people to retire there. But that doesn't mean you can't get a visa for New Zealand - far from it. The New Zealand government is keen to recruit qualified, skilled workers who will complement the economy. The immigration process works on a points system with points awarded according to your profession, experience, age and qualifications. You will need to lodge an 'Expression of interest (EIO)' to be considered. The main three routes to getting a visa being through the 'Skilled independent visa', 'Business visa' or 'Work to residence' scheme and the process can take up to nine months.

Dubai

Property development in Dubai has been heavily promoted in recent years and the property market has flattened out, with the usual problem of over development. The State of Dubai property boom was been largely the vision of one man, Sheikh

Mohammed Al-Maktoun who has worked in conjunction with British estate agents Savills. However, notwithstanding the miles and miles of development, new islands, celebrity endorsements and so on, it is very wise indeed to think carefully before investing in Dubai. The property market has experienced a crash since 2008 with many investors losing lots of money.

Although the country is not as problematic as some of its neighbours nevertheless it is in the middle east and as such there are political risks. The weather is very hot and there is a limited amount to do. Basically, the place is an artificial enclave, much like Las Vegas in its infancy without the liberal attitudes. Remember it is a Moslem country. There are many problems associated with Dubai and because of its culture the legal system and law of inheritance are complicated. There is no capital gains tax and little or no tax at all. It is possible to obtain mortgages on Dubai property but the set up costs are high. The development, although slowing down, still continues and it is predicted that Dubai will be a conference and holiday centre in years to come. Beware of predictions. There is a legal ban on females purchasing and inheriting real estate. However, 50% of foreign investors are female and so this ban could adversely affect the values of property. Think carefully and carry out exhaustive research before committing. With so much development there will be many inducements to buy.

The purchasing process

Buying property in Dubai is now much easier than it once was, thanks to the law allowing foreigners to buy freehold property. To buy a new-build off-plan (which most available property currently is) the process is fairly straightforward. The property buyer reserves a unit and pays an initial deposit-usually 10%. The remaining balance is paid in stages until the completion date. This varies with the developer and should be agreed before the deal.

For resale property, once you have found a property, a holding deposit is paid until funds are in place to carry out the exchange.

Although Dubai is tax free, you may find that you are required to pay taxes in the UK. You will certainly need professional advice before entering into a transaction.

Fees and taxes

For new-builds, expect land registration fees of around 2% and a years upfront maintenance charges, which will vary depending on the development. If buying a resale property, all the charges of a new build apply, plus a 1-2% transfer fee, depending on whether the property is complete.

Allow between 2-5% agents fees. While a lawyer is not legally required when buying a property in Dubai, it is advisable to get one to act for you.

Thailand

Before the Tsunami hit Thailand, islands such as Phuket were popular destinations for those seeking to buy property abroad. However, the number of foreign nationals buying in these areas has dwindled. People are still buying on the mainland, in places such as Chang Mai. Foreign nationals are allowed to own property but not land. Apartments are held leasehold with most leases being for 30 years. There is an option to renew after that time. If a man marries a Thai woman then he can buy property in her name only, and vice-versa. Strict building regulations apply. The majority of properties are being sold off plan. It is essential to make enquiries before buying an off plan property as sometimes the land is not in the legal ownership of the developer. Never part with any money before this has been established.

Hotspots

On the Thai mainland, Pattaya is one of Asia's largest beach resorts and the second most visited city in Thailand (after Bangkok, 150 kilometres north). The typical buyer in Pattaya is changing; from single males, drawn by its nightlife, to more families. In particular those younger visitors are visiting Jomtien, a few kilometres away, and wanting to experience Pattaya's floating markets and other cultural experiences. Houses in Pattaya range in value from 2 million baht to 50 million baht.

A typical house 15 minutes from the city centre would be 3 million baht, in a gated community with a communal swimming pool. Apartments run from less than 1 million baht all the way up to penthouses in excess of 80 million baht. You can buy a very nice apartment close to the beach from 1.2 million baht.

Meanwhile, on the other side of the Gulf of Thailand, 200 kilometres from Bangkok, is the country's oldest beach resort,

Hua Hin. Here, new residential and retail developments, as well as golf courses, are attracting an increasing number of buyers from Bangkok, as well as from Europe - and there's now a sizable community of expat Brits.

Forty-five minutes south of Hua Hin is the quiet beach village of Kuiburi where you can find boutique developments with access to the beach, private infinity pool, Jacuzzi and rooftop terrace.

Also consider its little sister, Koh Phangan. Given that 70 per cent of Koh Phangan is protected by national park status, the island should always maintain its unspoilt charm. On the west coast, idyllic properties with infinity pools can be found in Baan Tai for 15 million baht and at Bay Residence, you could take on a self-build villa project near the pretty bay of Haad Salad with plots starting at around £50,000.

With a larger budget, you could consider the natural eden of Yao Noi – 60 per cent of the island is covered in rainforest – where a one-bedroom villa will start at around £517,000; two- and three-bedroom options are available with prices reaching £800,000.

Buying process

Your solicitor will do most of the searches before you have to sign anything or pay any deposit - so ensure you take good legal advice if you're being asked to pay upfront. You will then pay a 10 per cent deposit. The final contract is signed when all the legal documents are ready, and at the same time you pay all relevant fees and taxes, and the deeds are registered with the Land Department.

Buying costs

In general, buyers pay around two per cent transfer fees, one per cent legal fees and 0.5 per cent stamp duty. Buying through a Thai company means you have to pay business tax of 3.3 per cent and if buying land, a local development tax.

Buyer Beware:

Under current Thai law foreigners are not allowed to purchase land freehold. It is however, possible to purchase a straightforward 90-year leasehold contract which provides the option to convert to freehold at any time, either should the law change, or should you wish to set up a company to buy the freehold title. This is the most common method that land is purchased in Thailand and a method fully endorsed by the Thai authorities. You will receive a 30-year lease with two subsequent renewal options, each of 30 years. A registered lease is easy to set up and there is no restriction on foreign participation. The standard Thailand residential lease is for 30 years and can be held in your own name. A lease registered with the Land Office remains in force during the term of each 30-year lease. After 30 years a new lease must be prepared and filed at the Land Office. Alternatively, you may convert the title to freehold. When you renew the lease there are no further payments to be made aside from a minimal local tax (approximately 1.1 per cent of the lease's value).The only exception to this rule is if you have a large sum to invest - Thailand has already allowed investors investing 40 million baht to own up to one rai (1,600 sq. metres or 0.4 acres) of land in certain areas.

****

Useful Information

Turkey

www.rightmove.co.uk/*overseas*-property/***in***-Turkey.*html*

*www.*turkey*homes.com/properties*

www.realestateinturkey.co.uk/

Brazil

www.propertyshowrooms.com/brazil/property/property

www.rightmove.co.uk/*overseas*-property/in-brazil

*the*brazil*business.com/article/how-to*-buy-*real-estate*-in-brazil

Morocco

www.gov.uk/guidance/buying-property-in-morocco

www.rightmove.co.uk/overseas-property/in-Morocco.html

www.globalpropertyguide.com/Middle-East/Morocco/Buying-Guide

South Africa

www.primelocation.com › International

www.globalpropertyguide.com/Africa/South-Africa/Buying-Guide

www.property-abroad.com/south-africa/buyers-guide

South African Property Overseas Marketing Association (SAPOA)

www.sapoa.org.za

Australia

www.realestate.com.au

www.realestatecentre.com.au

www.rightmove.co.uk/overseas-property/Australia-guide.html

First National Bank

www.firstnational.com.au

Gives advice on the financial aspects of relocating to Australia

New Zealand

www.rightmove.co.uk/overseas-property/New-Zealand-guide.html

www.globalpropertyguide.com/Pacific/New-Zealand/Buying-Guide

www.newzealandnow.govt.nz/living-in-nz/housing/buying-building

Dubai

www.damacproperties.com

www.wikihow.com/Buy-Property-in-Dubai

www.selectproperty.com/locations/uae-property/dubai

www.gov.uk/guidance/how-to-buy-property-in-the-uae

For information on financing a purchase in Dubai

www.katafinancial.com

167

www.aplaceinthesun.com/thailand

www.thailand-property.com

Phuket Property

www.phuketproperty.co.uk

www.globalpropertyguide.com/Asia/Thailand/Buying-Guide

www.expatfocus.com/thailand-property-culture-shock

Thailand Embassy

www.thaiembassy.com/thailand/buying-realestate-thailand.php

****

Buying a property abroad
Summary

You will have absorbed some of the main points related to investing in property abroad during the process of reading this book. Of necessity, this book, because of its wide range, has covered the main areas related to property acquisition. In order to reinforce those points, I have provided a summary below:

- Always, always **thoroughly** research the country of your choice before entering into any property transaction. Remember, developers and their agents are very keen to offload their properties and will offer any amount of inducements to the would-be purchaser. Look at climate, tourism, distance from the UK, are there regular flights and do budget airlines go there? What is the distance from the UK to the country of your choice and how feasible is it that you will use it as a regular holiday home. Look at potential for the future and look at rental possibilities and the long-term future.

- Once satisfied with your choice then research specific locations-what exactly do you want from an investment: Beach? Sports? Gated developments? List your wants and needs before investing.

- Ensure that you have a grip on the entire process of purchasing, from beginning to end and do try to read case studies on the internet or other books dealing specifically with the country of your choice before committing. As we have consistently mentioned, some legal systems, particularly in the tertiary countries are weak and there are inherent dangers. There are also problems in a number of countries with establishing title.

- Make sure that you have hired a good lawyer, bi-lingual, independent of all other parties, in particular developers and their agents.

- Make sure that you can raise all the finance to purchase a property and that you have a grip on the final running costs of the property, such as ongoing service charges. Make sure that you sort out the mortgage that is right for your future needs.

- Make sure that you are fully aware of tax implications of purchasing a property abroad, in particular the country of your choice.

- Make sure that you have a local will drawn up as soon as you have purchased a property. As we have seen some countries are more problematic than others, such as France for example, in relation to wills and inheritance.

****

Index

www.straightforwardco.co.uk

All Titles listed below, in the Straightforward Guides Series can be purchased online, using credit card or other forms of payment by going to www.straightfowardco.co.uk A discount of 25% per title is offered with online purchases.

Law

A Straightforward Guide to:

Consumer Rights

Bankruptcy Insolvency and the Law

Employment Law

Private Tenants Rights

Family law

Small Claims in the County Court

Contract law

Intellectual Property and the law

Divorce and the law

Leaseholders Rights

The Process of Conveyancing

Knowing Your Rights and Using the Courts

Producing Your own Will

Housing Rights

The Bailiff the law and You

Probate and The Law

Company law

What to Expect When You Go to Court

Guide to Competition Law

Give me Your Money-Guide to Effective Debt Collection

Caring for a Disabled Child

General titles

Letting Property for Profit

Buying, Selling and Renting property

Buying a Home in England and France

Bookkeeping and Accounts for Small Business

Creative Writing

Freelance Writing

Writing Your own Life Story

Writing performance Poetry

Writing Romantic Fiction

Speech Writing

Teaching Your Child to Read and write

Creating a Successful Commercial Website

The Straightforward Business Plan

The Straightforward C.V.

Successful Public Speaking

Handling Bereavement

Individual and Personal Finance

Understanding Mental Illness

The Two Minute Message

Go to: www.straightforwardco.co.uk